Interpreting Test Scores

David Monroe Miller

B.F.S. Psychological Associates, Inc.

John Wiley & Sons

New York · London · Sydney

Copyright © 1972, by John Wiley & Sons, Inc.

All rights reserved. Published simultaneously in Canada.

No part of this book may be reproduced by any means, nor transmitted, nor translated into a machine language without the written permission of the publisher.

Library of Congress Cataloging in Publication Data

Miller, David Monroe, 1940–
    Interpreting test scores.

    (Wiley self-teaching guides)
    Bibliography: p.
    1. Educational tests and measurements. 2. Mental tests. I. Title
LB1131.M57   371.2'6   72-4530
ISBN 0-471-60609-X

Printed in the United States of America.

72   73   10 9 8 7 6 5 4 3 2 1

Preface

The interpretation of test scores underlies many important questions in education, psychology, employment, and public policy. Do intelligence tests unfairly discriminate against the underprivileged? How large a part should test results play in college admissions? Is <u>one</u> test a sufficient basis for making an important educational or career decision? Should parents know their child's score on an intelligence test?

This introductory book does not attempt to answer all these questions. Some will not even be discussed. The goal, rather, is to give the student—or teacher, parent, personnel manager, or school administrator—the necessary technical and commonsense background to be able to enter into the debate or to do advanced reading on his own.

Another goal of this book is to provide the reader with the basic statistical concepts that must be understood before any of the broader questions relating to tests can be considered. The concepts of mean, standard deviation, normal distribution, correlation coefficient, and standard error are necessary not only for the psychology or education major, but also for the practicing teacher or concerned parent. The book assumes <u>no</u> prior knowledge of these concepts and requires only the most elementary arithmetical operations. Readers who are already familiar with basic statistical concepts will have the opportunity to skip certain indicated sections.

To meet the needs of a wide variety of readers, the chapters have been arranged so that they can be read independently of one another. For example, the graduate student in psychology may wish to place highest priority on Chapters 4 and 5—"Validity" and "Reliability"; however, readers who find that these two chapters are outside their current interest may skip them at the first reading and return to them when they are ready for more advanced work. Professional educators or other readers who are highly experienced in working with standardized tests of educational achievement may skim Chapter 1 and begin serious work with Chapter 2.

The Chapter Objectives describe what the reader should be able to do after completing each chapter. A test at the end of each chapter reflects these objectives, giving the reader the opportunity to review and apply what was learned in the chapter. The chapter tests can be used as a self-pacing guide. The reader should look at the test before beginning each chapter, and if he can <u>easily</u> answer <u>most</u> of the test questions, he may skip that chapter or skim through it.

The Final Examination covers all the chapter objectives and also requires the reader to discriminate among the various concepts introduced in the book. The reader who has gone through all six chapters and the chapter tests should be able to answer correctly at least 90 percent of the questions in the Final Examination.

Interpreting Test Scores was designed to be completely self-instructional, although it can also be used by students enrolled in courses.

David Monroe Miller

New York, N. Y.
September 1972

Acknowledgments

John Wiley and Sons, Inc., has been helpful in supplying reference material and in allowing reproduction of copyrighted excerpts. Ms. Judy Vantrease Wilson, editor of the Wiley Self-Teaching Guides Series, has provided invaluable advice and encouragement.

The Houghton Mifflin Company, Inc., has generously permitted reproduction of copyrighted materials appearing on pages 126 and 132.

The professional staff of B.F.S. Psychological Associates, Inc., has been helpful to me in many ways. Special acknowledgement is made to Dr. Mortimer R. Feinberg, President, and Mr. Myron Katz, Project Director.

Significant editorial contributions have been made by Mss. Thelma Baer, Irene Brownstone, Elizabeth Ross-Miller, and Sif Wiksten.

Mrs. Ann Ross, Chief of the Sociology and Education Division of the Washington, D. C., Public Library, has assisted me in obtaining publications and has reviewed portions of the manuscript.

Mrs. Sylvia Miller has been indispensable as an editorial and administrative assistant. This book could not have been written without her help.

Professors Joseph P. Gutkoska of Towson State College in Maryland and Samuel T. Mayo of Loyola University in Chicago have read earlier drafts of the book and offered many useful suggestions. Neither they nor any of the other persons mentioned, however, are responsible for any errors that may appear.

D. M. M.

Note to Students

Interpreting Test Scores may be of special interest to students in college or graduate-level courses in education and psychology. This book is not intended to substitute for a comprehensive textbook; rather, it is designed to give the student the necessary background to be able to get more out of his textbook and his course. In particular:

> The basic statistical concepts can serve as a refresher for students who have had an introductory course in statistics some years ago, or as new material for students who do not need a complete statistics course but do require an understanding of the statistical basis for interpreting test scores.

> The chapters on Validity and Reliability contain indispensable "foundation material" for students in any psychology course at the graduate level (although personality assessment is not directly covered).

> Throughout this book there is a constant attempt to sort out the various issues involved in tests and measurements—technical, moral, judgmental, statistical.

> Students will be better prepared to benefit from a course using one or more of the textbooks listed on pages 149-150, Suggestions for Additional Reading, as a result of reading this book.

Note to Instructors

In order to determine how this book might be helpful to your students, the recommended procedure is to scan the Chapter Objectives, listed on pages ix-x, and look at the chapter tests and the final Examination which reflect these objectives.

If the objectives of this book are also the <u>terminal</u> objectives of your course, you could use this book as a supplement to your regular textbook, assigning it on a chapter-by-chapter basis in any order. However, if the objectives of this book are actually prerequisites to your own course, <u>Interpreting Test Scores</u> should be assigned to be read straight through at the beginning of the course. One or two weeks should be allowed. If assigned on a chapter-by-chapter basis, each chapter, including the test, should require between one and two hours.

How to Use This Book

Each chapter is divided into numbered "frames." In each frame, information is presented and the reader is given a question to answer or an exercise to do. The frame ends with a dotted line, below which is found the correct answer (or several possible correct answers).

Many of the frames call not only for an answer, but also for the reasoning behind the answer. It is important to write—not simply think—both the answer and your underlying reasoning (if that is what is asked for).

While you are reading the frame, use an index card or a note pad to cover the answers that appear below the frame (after the dotted line). You should usually be able to answer correctly if you have taken the time to read the material and carefully think about your answer. You will discover that many of your answers can be considered correct even if they do not exactly match the suggested answers in the book. If you find that your analysis of a problem was only partially correct, change your answer for future reference.

Each chapter should be read at a single sitting. If it is necessary to stop before the end of a chapter, try to do so at one of the suggested "break points" indicated in each chapter.

Chapter Objectives

CHAPTER 1   REFERENCE POPULATIONS AND NORMS

After completing this chapter, the student will be able to

(1) define and/or give examples of "reference population," "standardization sample," and "norm";
(2) recognize a "raw score" and state what needs to be known before the raw score is interpretable;
(3) define "measurement error" nontechnically and show how it may affect interpretation of test scores;
(4) define "mean" and "median" and compute either one from a set of sample data;
(5) find relevant information in a typical norms table;
(6) show how "grade equivalents" and "age equivalents" may be misleading;
(7) distinguish between conclusions that can and cannot legitimately be drawn from a test score, and suggest appropriate qualifications and reservations for those that are uncertain.

CHAPTER 2   PERCENTILE RANKS AND STANDARD SCORES

After completing this chapter, the student will be able to

(1) define percentile rank and show how it is dependent on the concept of "reference population";
(2) show that most verbal descriptions of abilities or characteristics are actually based on a percentile ranking within a normal distribution;
(3) recognize how the interpretation of a test score depends on the mean result and the standard deviation about the mean;
(4) given a person's score on a test, the mean, and the standard deviation, compute the person's z score;
(5) convert a z score into a percentile rank by means of (a) an educated guess based on the properties of the normal distribution, and (b) properly using a table;
(6) interpret scores on College Board Examinations in accordance with the statistical concepts mentioned above.

CHAPTER 3   IQ SCORES

After completing this chapter, the student will be able to

(1) distinguish between "Intelligence Quotient" and "deviation IQ score";

    (2) apply all the objectives of Chapters 1 and 2 to standardized tests of general intelligence, with particular emphasis on the Stanford-Binet, Wechsler, and Lorge-Thorndike tests;

    (3) show the importance and implications of distinguishing between "verbal" and "nonverbal" components of an IQ score;

    (4) show that a deviation IQ score is simply a percentile rank within a given reference population;

    (5) given a typical computerized reporting form for a class of 17 students, be able to (a) understand the meaning of the figures and (b) judge which are of special significance;

    (6) show the pitfalls involved in applying verbal labels to IQ scores.

CHAPTER 4   VALIDITY

After completing this chapter, the student will be able to

    (1) show that it is inappropriate to consider a test as "valid" or "invalid" without taking into account (a) the purpose of the test and (b) the aspect of validity under consideration;

    (2) distinguish between face validity, criterion-related validity, content validity, and construct validity;

    (3) show how correlation coefficients are used to assess criterion-related validity;

    (4) given diagrams indicating positive, zero, and negative correlations, identify and briefly give the meaning of each;

    (5) given some hypothetical validity studies, briefly discuss the procedures and results.

CHAPTER 5   RELIABILITY

After completing this chapter, the student will be able to

    (1) define reliability in terms of consistency and show how it is an inherent problem in any measuring procedure;

    (2) briefly define the three major methods of estimating reliability (test-retest, alternate-form, and split-half), and indicate the circumstances in which one might be a better method than others;

    (3) define and give examples of practice and fatigue effects;

    (4) show why reliability coefficients should be higher than validity coefficients.

CHAPTER 6   STANDARD ERROR OF MEASUREMENT

After completing this chapter, the student will be able to

    (1) from a commonsense point of view, explain what is meant by "95 percent confidence interval";

    (2) given a reliability coefficient and the standard deviation of a test, compute the standard error of measurement for that test;

    (3) given the above, compute a 95 percent confidence interval around the observed score;

    (4) distinguish between "observed score" and "true score," and show why the latter has to be hypothetical;

    (5) show how decisions might be affected by taking into account the standard error of measurement;

    (6) Review some of the objectives in earlier chapters.

Contents

CHAPTER ONE
Reference Populations and Norms

1.   In the Preface we mentioned just a few of the controversial issues
in education and psychology that relate to the interpretation of test
scores. The reason so many questions can be asked--along with doz-
ens of others that have not yet reached the public-controversy stage--
is that measurement, far from being a totally exact and objective procedure, is based on certain assumptions that are impossible to verify
with 100 percent certainty. Thus we always have to ask: "What conclusions can we draw from a given result, on what grounds, and with
what degree of certainty?"

Suppose, for example, we measure the height of John Williams, a
16-year-old boy, and obtain a result of 79 inches (6'7"). Which of the
following conclusions do you think could be reasonably drawn from the
result?*

_____ John's actual height is 79 inches
_____ John is very tall
_____ He is more likely than most boys his
        age to be successful at basketball
_____ He is more likely than most boys his
        age to be a good dancer
_____ He is probably better at arithmetic
        than most boys his age

- - - - - - - - - - - - - - - - - - - -

_____ John's actual height is 79 inches
_____ John is very tall
_____ He is more likely than most boys his
        age to be successful at basketball

(If your answer was different, the rest of the book may indicate that
you were actually right--or show why you were wrong.)

2.   Let's consider just the first conclusion--that John's actual height
is 79 inches. This should mean that any time we measure him we
would get the same result. But we know from experience that even if
the same person using the same tape measure only a minute later were

---

*Note: Many questions in this book will be in this format. Check any
that you consider correct--including all of them or none of them, if
that is what you think.

to measure John again, it is quite likely that a different result, such as 78 1/2 or 79 1/16 inches, would be obtained.

The fact that measurement results <u>tend to vary</u> is an extremely important principle in testing. There are many tangible reasons which might account for the variation--even though we might never know which ones are operating in any given case. What are some circumstances that might lead to a different result the next time we measure John?

_____

_____

- -

He might not stand up as straight ... tape measure might not be pulled as taut or held as straight ... the head angle of the person reading the measurement might be slightly different ... (and so on)

3.   Any or all of these circumstances--and possibly a few more that you might have thought of--could contribute to <u>measurement error.</u> The word "error," as used in the field of tests and measurements, may be misleading. It does not mean that a mistake was made; it simply refers to the deviation between the actual value and the result that we obtain on any given measurement.

Suppose, then, that Betty takes an intelligence test and obtains a certain score. A week later she takes the same test. Assume that she has not discovered the correct answers in the interim, that her intelligence has not changed in a week, and that no mechanical errors were made in scoring either test. Nonetheless we could still predict that in all probability her score the second time will be somewhat different. What might account for this?

_____

_____

_____

- -

How much sleep she had the night before ... what kind of breakfast she had ... how she felt about the person administering the test ... distractions in the testing situation ... (and undoubtedly many other possibilities)

4.   Of course, just from looking at the result, we never know which (if any) of these factors were operating, and to what degree they may have affected the result. What we do know is that measurement error is inevitable. Thus, in order to draw the proper conclusions from a test result, we need some way of estimating the probably amount of error in any given case. In Chapter 6 we will study this problem and

show how to compute the amount of measurement error that you can expect from some well-known tests.

In review, <u>measurement error</u> refers to:

_____ the difference between an actual value and the result obtained on any given test

_____ mistakes made in scoring or administering a test

- -

_____ the difference between an actual value and the result obtained on any given test

5.   In our first example, we concluded from the result of 79 inches that John's actual height is, in fact, 79 inches. Given the inevitability of some degree of measurement error, would you still hold to this conclusion? (YES/NO)

If you said YES, what qualifications or reservations would you have?

_____

_____

_____

- -

Yes, we could still conclude that John's actual height is 79 inches--but only if we qualify it. You might have said that this conclusion is subject to a certain amount of measurement error, or that it is only a probability rather than a certainty, or that we might have to measure John several more times.

6.   Now let's look at the second conclusion in frame 1--that John is a very tall person. What are some possible grounds for this conclusion?

_____

_____

- -

(Answer is discussed below.)

7.   Whatever words you may have chosen, they would probably amount to one of the following, or both:

79 inches is considerably above the average height of boys this age

there are relatively few boys this age who are 79 inches or taller

However, if John were a member of the Watusi tribe, in which heights of 7 feet are not at all uncommon, then neither of the above statements would be true. Any conclusion that contains an adjective, such as "very tall," "superior in intellectual ability," "deficient in reading comprehension," etc. implies a comparison of the individual with some reference population.

A reference population may be defined in terms of age, sex, socioeconomic status, geographic location, or whatever you consider relevant to the particular characteristic that is being measured or tested. In the reference population "16-year-old American boys," 79 inches is undoubtedly "very" tall, but 72 inches (6 feet) probably isn't. Name some reference populations in which 72 inches would be considered "very tall."

_____

_____

- -

females
Asians
persons under 14 (or some other age)
prehistoric humans
(Or many other answers, as discussed below)

8.   Since a reference population can be whatever you define it to be, you could have suggested others, or some very narrow ones such as "females under 14 in North Korea." But whatever you did answer, it is clear that the concept of "very tall" will change its meaning depending on the reference population. The same is true for anything we measure in education or psychology.

In the height example, reference populations could be defined in terms of age, sex, geographic location, and even time period in history, simply because we have good grounds for believing that all these factors are relevant to differences in height.

In most educational measurements, our interest is usually in age, grade in school, and/or sex. Age and grade, of course, are very closely related to one another but it is often worthwhile to distinguish between them. In general, if we are measuring something that was learned primarily in school, it would make more sense to define the reference group in terms of (AGE/GRADE). If we are measuring something that is the result of family factors, physical maturity, or other nonschool causes, then we would be more interested in (AGE/GRADE).

(Circle AGE or GRADE in each of the two places.)

- -

GRADE
AGE

9.   We are interpreting some test results of Joseph, a fourth grader, age 9 1/2. Next to each of the following indicate whether the results would be more meaningful when compared to other children of Joseph's age, or others of Joseph's grade, based on the discussion in the preceding frame.

_____ athletic ability
_____ reading ability
_____ arithmetical ability

- - - - - - - - - - - - - - - - - - - -

athletic ability: age (because it is not learned in school)
reading ability: grade
arithmetical ability: grade

10.   In deciding whether or not to include sex in our definition of a particular reference group, we need to know the extent to which sex differences actually exist. There are two ways to approach this question. One is by a purely logical analysis. We know, for example, that athletic ability depends to some extent on muscular structure which is different in boys and girls. Thus we would either give entirely different tests to boys and girls, or else give the same test but interpret the results of any individual only with reference to others of his or her own sex.
      Another way to approach the question of sex differences is through statistical rather than logical analysis. Differences do exist in some areas, even if we do not know what factors (biological, social, psychological, etc.) might account for them. For example, there is ample research to indicate that girls generally do better than boys at all school subjects in the elementary grades, but that these differences gradually disappear.
      If you were interpreting Barbara's result on a statewide reading test, which reference population would you compare her to? (Barbara is 7 1/2 years old and in the second grade.)

_____ 7 1/2-year-old girls
_____ second-grade children
_____ second-grade girls
_____ second-grade children of Barbara's age

- - - - - - - - - - - - - - - - - - - -

second-grade girls (The relevant characteristics are grade, because reading is learned primarily in school, and sex, because girls generally do better than boys early in school. However, since no direct evidence was presented, you can consider yourself correct if you answered "second-grade children.")

11.   We might also be interested in comparing a given result to the scores of the other children in the same classroom. When the test is the teacher's own test, then of course no other comparisons are possible. When the test is standardized--one that is the same for all

persons in a large geographical area--then the individual classroom is not a suitable reference population for drawing a general conclusion about an individual.

Suppose, for example, that in a standardized arithmetic achievement test Edgar ranks fourth out of 31 in his class, but that his result is only about average for all boys in his grade on a nationwide basis. It would be entirely proper to conclude that Edgar needs less work in arithmetic than most of the other children in his class. This may be useful to know for planning purposes. The general conclusion to draw about Edgar's arithmetic ability, however, insofar as we can do it from this one result, is that it is (SUPERIOR/AVERAGE).

- -

AVERAGE

12.   This discussion is not meant to imply that the purpose of educational measurement is to enable us to apply adjectives to people. The fact is, however, that judgments, comparative statements, adjectives, or conclusions of one kind or another are always being used. The point is not to eliminate them, but to make sure of our grounds for using them, and to evaluate the degree of certainty we have about them.

In order to achieve these goals we have to understand the mathematical significance of any given result. As a first step, we have to compare an individual with a given reference population. In general, a reference population consists of:

_____ all persons who have ever taken the test
_____ all persons who share certain specified characteristics
_____ the individual's own class in school

- -

_____ all persons who share certain specified characteristics (The other answers are not incorrect, because being in the same classroom or having taken the same test could also be considered "certain specified characteristics." However, the above answer is the most general one.)

13.   Before we can make meaningful comparisons within a reference population, we have to know the meaning of the score itself. When we measure John and obtain a result of 79 inches, 79 could be considered his "score." We have no trouble in understanding what the number means, because we know what an inch is. It has the same meaning no matter what is being measured, and it can be visualized.

When we make nonphysical measurements--as in the vast majority of tests that are used--our initial results are expressed not in inches, but in points. Does one point have the same meaning on every test? (YES/NO) Can we visualize what a "point is? (YES/NO)

- -

NO
NO

14.   Suppose that Alice scores 18 on an arithmetic test. The number of points itself, known as the raw score, tells us nothing. Did she answer 18 questions correctly? Not necessarily; she may have answered one 10-point question, two 4-point questions, and missed everything else. What information would you need to get a feel for the numerical significance of the raw score (18 in this example)?

_____ what grade the student is in
_____ the average score on this test
_____ the highest possible score
        (assume that the lowest is zero)
_____ the subject matter of the test
_____ the number of questions on the test

- - - - - - - - - - - - - - - - - - - -

_____ the average score on this test
_____ the highest possible score

15.   If you checked any of the others, ask yourself the significance of a score of 72 on a ninth-grade English test containing 14 questions. There's no way to begin answering unless you know at least one of the other two pieces of information listed above.
        If we know the highest possible score, we can transform the raw score into a percentage. For example, if the highest possible score were 20, then 18 would represent 90 percent. This means that the student can do 90 percent of the work:

_____ required on that test
_____ covered in the course
_____ in the subject matter at his grade level
_____ in the subject matter as a whole

- - - - - - - - - - - - - - - - - - - -

_____ required on the test
(Some of the others may be true, but we arrived at the 90 percent figure only by computing the score on this test.)

16.   This tells us more than the raw score itself, but even the percentage still leaves a lot of information lacking and is open to misinterpretation. For one thing, people often have illusions about numbers that tend to make 90 percent seem much better than 89 percent, while the difference between, say, 91 percent and 90 percent seems negligible. There is no direct way to attack this habit of thinking except by becoming familiar with other types of scoring systems, such as those discussed later in this book.
        Another and more basic problem with either raw scores or percentages is that they are not comparable, or only partially so, with scores made on other tests. For example, if Billy gets a score of 74 percent in an algebra exam and 83 percent in a French exam, the algebra score might actually be "better." For one thing, 74 percent in algebra might represent a very marked improvement over his own

previous performance. Give one or two other reasons why a score of 74 percent in one test might actually be better than a score of 83 percent in another test.

_____

_____

- -

The algebra test might have been more difficult than the French test. This is not easy to prove just from looking at the tests--but any student can tell the difference!

Another answer, which to some extent incorporates the first one, is that the 74 percent score might actually have been, say, the third best in the class, while in the French class a dozen students might have scored over 90 percent.

Even when a score is a percentage, then, we need to know, at a minimum, how difficult the test is and how the score stands in relation to other scores that were actually achieved. When dealing with just the raw score itself, we also need to know the highest and lowest possible scores on the test.

We can short-cut the need for much of the above information if we know the average score. The concept of "average" can be defined in several different ways. We will discuss only the two most common-- the median and the arithmetic mean. If you are familiar with these concepts you can skip right now to frame 19 on page 9.

17.   The arithmetic mean (usually referred to simply as the "mean") is the "average" as most of us first learned it--totaling the scores and dividing by the number of scores. Suppose we have a 20-word spelling test, with the results as shown below. The sum is 140, so the mean is _____ .

Alice	17
Barbara	15
Charles	4
Daniel	18
Elsa	19
Francis	10
Gerry	3
Howard	15
Irene	20
James	19
	140

- -

14 (the sum, 140, divided by the number of scores, 10)

18.   The purpose of an average is to give a general picture of a "typical" result. Does 14 really do this job? Seven out of the 10 students
have scored <u>above</u> 14, so perhaps it does not describe the "typical"
result.
        Another way to look at the data is to focus on the value that ranks
in the middle. This is known as the <u>median</u>. To find the median, we
first have to rank the scores in order. This has been done below (using the same data as in the previous example). Since there is an even
number of scores (10), there is no one middle value. As indicated by
the bar, the median is between the fifth score (17) and the sixth score
(15). To establish the median value we take the mean of those two
midpoints--that is, we "split the difference" and arrive at _____ as
our median value.

Irene	20
Elsa	19
James	19
Daniel	18
Alice	17
Barbara	15
Howard	15
Francis	10
Charles	4
Gerry	3

- -

16

19.   Given the following scores, what is the mean? _____. What
is the median? _____.

12
6
11
7
4

- -

mean: 8 (40 ÷ 5)
median: 7 (the middle-ranking score)
(If you were incorrect and originally skipped this section, go back to
frame 17.)

20.   When dealing with a small number of persons--say, no more than
one classroom--the median is about as simple to calculate as the mean
and is a better way of dividing the class into two groups. It usually
gives a slightly better picture of the "average" score, especially if
there are a few extreme values that obviously do not fall within the
general pattern of scores.

When we are concerned with <u>larger</u> numbers of persons, the mean is generally a more accurate representation of the average, is easier to calculate, and can be used in some general formulas which are helpful in interpreting results. The reasons for these statements are beyond our scope. Any elementary statistics textbook will discuss in more detail the mean and the median, together with the "mode" and other measures of "average."

As a review, compute the mean and median of the following scores:

$$20$$
$$25$$
$$11$$
$$14$$
$$8$$
$$12$$

- -

mean: 15 $(90 \div 6)$
median: 13 (splitting the difference between 14 and 12)

(<u>Here is the best break point in this chapter.</u>)

21.   In a classroom test--one that is designed by a teacher for use in his own classroom--there is little problem in understanding the raw scores, since the teacher is fully familiar with the content of the test, the scoring system used, the highest and lowest scores (possible and actual), the average score (if he computes it), and the past perform-ance of individual pupils.

In a standardized test, on the other hand, the raw-score figures have no meaning at all at first glance. We can interpret them only with the aid of <u>norms</u> provided by the test publisher.

A norm is the average score achieved by any given reference pop-ulation. Usually the average is the mean, rather than the median, but for our purposes it makes no difference.

Suppose, then, that on a nationwide test of reading ability, the average raw score achieved by all seventh graders is 49 points. In this example, then, 49 is the seventh-grade norm. It is important to understand, from the definition itself and from the example, that 49 is the score that:

_____   <u>should be</u> achieved by a person in the seventh grade
_____   <u>has been</u> achieved by seventh graders

- -

<u>has been</u> achieved by seventh graders

22.   It is important to keep in mind that the norm is a statement of what other persons <u>have done</u>. The average score of 49 in this hypo-thetical example was computed by giving the test to a sample of seventh

graders (and students from all grades, but our example happens to focus on the seventh grade). The sample, known as the <u>standardization
sample</u>, might consist of thousands of students. These students are
selected to represent the entire country--at the time the norms are
computed and for some years after that.

Suppose, for example, that Carl scores 75 on a standardized
reading test. The average score of all students at his grade level,
according to the norms table in the test manual, is 73. Looking in the
test manual, you discover that the norms were computed on a standardization sample in 1962.

Let's suppose that the test itself has not been changed since 1962,
but that better teaching methods have caused the general level of reading ability in the nation to rise since 1962. In that case, Carl's score,
apparently 2 points above the average, might actually be (LESS/MORE)
than 2 points above average.

- -

LESS (as explained below)

23.   If the general level of reading ability has risen, then the average
score on the test would have risen from 73 to some higher number.
In that case Carl's score of 75 might actually turn out to be average
or below average. In order to know we would need an updated standardization sample.

In practice, this is not a real problem. Test publishers do, in
fact, revise and update their norms tables, their tests, or both. Moreover, as we will see later, a difference of a few points one way or the
other is not likely to be important. The point is that the norm was
computed on the basis of a standardization sample which is supposed to
be representative of the entire reference population. You can usually
assume that this is the case, but any time you use a published norms
table it is wise to read the introductory material to the table which
should describe the composition of the standardization sample.

For a more detailed discussion of this point, see Anastasi (1968,
cited in bibliography), pp. 63-64, or most other texts, looking under
the topics "standardization," "standardization sample," or "norms."

(<u>No answer necessary.</u>)

24.   Exhibit 1 on page 126 shows some norms data for a widely used
standardized intelligence test. The discussion of this table and the
concept of norm in general applies to all tests, not just intelligence
tests.

Notice that the table gives ages and grades to the nearest month.
For example, age 7-11 means 7 years and 11 months. The grade lev-
els are given to the nearest tenth of a year, which is actually equivalent to about a month.

As you can see, this table does not show separate norms for the
two sexes. We can assume, then, that in the original standardization
sample it was verified statistically that a person's sex (IS/IS NOT)

related to his or her performance on this test.

_ _

IS NOT
(Unless otherwise noted, in the rest of this book we will assume that
this is the case in all examples we use.)

25.　　Still referring to Exhibit 1, suppose we want to know the average
score of children 9 years and 1 month of age. (In practice we would
probably use a different table to get this information, but this one will
still serve the purpose.) Looking to the left of age 9-1, we see that
the average score, to the nearest whole number, is _____ points.

_ _

51

26.　　Suppose now that we were interested in students in the sixth month
of the fourth grade. Looking up the table under Grade 4.6, we see two
entries. (Ignore the ages 9-10 and 9-11, which are of no interest for
the moment.) Continuing to read to the left of 4.6, we see that the
raw-score average for this reference population (Grade 4.6) must be
somewhere between 64 and _____.

_ _

65

27.　　If we wanted to know the average more precisely, we would use a
different table. The purpose of this particular table is to enable us to
tell what the scores themselves mean, so we start with the score we
are interested in and then read the information to the right of the
score.
　　　　Suppose, for example, that Lois, age 8 1/2 and in the middle of
the third grade, obtains a score of 72 on this test. Looking to the
right of this score, we find that it is the average score obtained by
students who are _____ (what age ?) and who are in _____
_____ (what grade ?)

_ _

10-4 (10 years and 4 months)
5.1 (first month of fifth grade)

28.　　As you can see from the headings in the table, these numbers are
referred to as age and grade "equivalents." This is a misleading
term, but since it is widely used it is important to be familiar with it.
Lois has scored 72. Let's just consider the age equivalent, 10-4.
Based on what we have said about norms, what does it actually mean
to say that 10-4 is the "age equivalent" for Lois's score of 72?

_____ 72 is the average score attained
by children of age 10-4
_____ Lois, who is 8 1/2, has done as well on this
test as the average child of age 10-4
_____ She is as intelligent as the average
child of age 10-4

- -

All can be considered correct, but all must be qualified somewhat as
discussed in the next two frames.

29.   The first choice in the preceding frame is correct. This is what
the table tells us (remembering that this is based on the standardization sample). The second statement is also correct since it is basically a reworded statement of the first. It should be kept in mind, however, that the phrase "average child" is actually shorthand for "the
average score obtained by children of this age." There is really no
such thing as an "average" child except in this statistical sense. We
will return to the sometimes-overlooked distinction between the person and the person's score later, in connection with our discussion of
IQ scores.
       Notice, also, that the statement was confined to this test. Lois
may, in fact, do as well as the average child of 10-4 on many different intelligence tests. Is this something we can conclude from the
norms table itself? (YES/NO)

- -

NO (the table only gives the average results on this particular test)

30.   The third statement in frame 28, "she is as intelligent as the average child of age 10-4," would be correct only with the reservations
just discussed; namely, that "more intelligent" has to be qualified by
"as measured by this test," and that "average child" is shorthand. We
don't know anything about the average child; what we do know from the
norms table is the average _____ obtained by children of this
age.

- -

score

31.   Summarizing thus far, Lois, an 8 1/2-year-old in the middle of
the third grade, attained a score of 72 on this intelligence test, which
is equal to the average score obtained by students approximately two
years older (10-4). Given that information, which of the following
conclusions would you draw?

Under each one, jot down your reasons for accepting it or rejecting it, or indicate what additional information you would like to have or assumptions you would have to make.*

_____ Lois is more intelligent than most children of her own age

_____

_____

_____ She can function as well as many 10-year-olds in all situations requiring intelligence

_____

_____

_____ She could skip at least one year in school without difficulty

_____

_____

- -

(Answers are discussed below.)

32.   The results themselves do not justify any of the statements, but together with certain assumptions a case can be made for accepting all of them. On the other hand, other assumptions might lead to rejecting some or even all of them.

To accept any of the conclusions, we have to assume that this particular test actually measures intelligence. Even then, we cannot automatically accept any of the conclusions without additional assumptions.

Consider the first statement in the preceding frame--that Lois is more intelligent than most children of her own age, based on the fact that her score was equal to the norm for students two years older. This requires the assumption that the average child of age 10-4 is more intelligent than the average child of 8-6 (Lois's age). This happens to be true with regard to intelligence in this age range. But it is not true at all age ranges and in regard to all qualities we may test.

Suppose, for example, that on a test of physical reflexes, a 40-year-old man were to attain a score equivalent to the average 50-year-old man. Based on what we can reasonably assume about physical reflexes, we would conclude that the 40-year-old has done (BETTER/WORSE) than the average man of his own age.

_____

*Note: For purposes of this exercise, do not worry about measurement error. That is, assume that the score of 72 is the same score Lois would get if she were tested several times.

- -

WORSE (In other words, 40-year-olds generally do better on reflex tests than 50-year-olds; 8 1/2-year-olds generally <u>do not</u> do better on intelligence tests than 10-year-olds.)

33.   The last two statements in frame 31 <u>may</u> be correct, but they are dubious conclusions to draw from the information given. The only "situations requiring intelligence" on which we know that Lois could function as well as many 10-year-olds are test-taking situations, and only in regard (as far as we know) to this particular intelligence test. Could she read as well, do the same kind of arithmetic problems, and remain undistracted at a mental task for as long a period of time as the average 10-year-old? Possibly, but probably not.

   For these reasons, and for many reasons having to do with personality and physical development, it would also be incorrect to conclude that Lois could skip a grade "without difficulty." Again, it <u>might</u> be true, but we would probably need more evidence.

   You might have rejected this choice on a much narrower ground-- that 10.4 is an age-equivalent score, not a grade equivalent. However, it had already been mentioned (or you could have looked up the table again) that the grade equivalent for a score of 72 is 5.1. Based on the above reasoning, could we assume that Lois (who is now in the third grade) can do fifth-grade work at this time? (YES/NO)

- -

NO

34.   Grade equivalents are open to the same reservations as age equivalents, and to some others besides. A child in the third grade, no matter how well developed physically, emotionally, or intellectually, could not do fifth-grade arithmetic involving fractions if he had not yet had any introduction to fractions.

   This would be true even if Lois's grade equivalent on an <u>arithmetic</u> test turned out to be 5.1. To illustrate this point, consider a standardized arithmetic achievement test designed to cover the entire elementary-school arithmetic curriculum, grades 3 through 6.

   Part of this hypothetical test consists of adding, subtracting, multiplying, and dividing with whole numbers; part consists of doing the same with decimals and fractions; part consists of problems in which these operations have to be used and the student has to know what needs to be done. (We are confining ourselves to the "old math" in this example.)

   Suppose that the raw scores range from 0 to 150. The third-grade norm (average) is 71; the fifth-grade average is 96. Lois does very well on the first two-thirds of the test, scoring 98 points. On the rest of the test she is completely stumped.

Meanwhile, Charles, a student in the fifth grade, misses many of the easy arithmetic problems but does fairly well in the more advanced sections of the test. His total score turns out to be 95, one point below the fifth-grade norm and 3 points below Lois.

Who is better equipped to do fifth-grade work in arithmetic?

_____ Lois
_____ Charles
_____ They would do equally well

- -

Charles (fifth-grade work will consist mainly of those things that Lois can't do at all)

35.   We have given some of the objections to the concept of age and grade "equivalents." Are there any positive ways in which they can be used? Probably not. In all of the textbooks cited in the Suggestions for Additional Reading, the objections and reservations are stated, but no positive use can be found. You may wish to examine the following:

> Anastasi, pp. 60-62
> Cronbach, pp. 385-387 (2nd edition), p. 98 (3rd edition)
> Lyman, pp. 112-118, especially pp. 115-118
> Thorndike and Hagen, pp. 214-219

We suggest, then, that for "age (or grade) equivalent," you substitute the words "age (or grade) at which this raw score is the average, based on the standardization sample."

This does not mean that norms tables are useless. On the contrary, without them we cannot begin to make sense of the raw scores. The point to keep in mind, however, is that it makes more sense to interpret a person's performance in terms of:

_____ how his score stands in relation to other ages and grades
_____ how he stands in relation to his own age or grade

- -

how he stands in relation to his own age or grade (or other reference-population characteristics in addition to age and grade)

36.   The statistical significance of a score within a given reference population will be the subject of the next chapter. The following questions will serve as a review of the material covered so far. Answers are on page 18.

TEST FOR CHAPTER 1

1. Compute the mean and the median of the following scores:

   6
   22
   19
   11
   14
   18

2. Karl scores 90 on an arithmetic test and 75 on an English test. Under what circumstances might his score of 75 be better than his score of 90?

   _____

   _____

   _____

3. In the preceding problem, the score of 75 (or the score of 90) would be an example of a:

   raw score
   norm
   median
   mean

4. Ellen, age 11-5 in the sixth grade, gets 85 questions right on a standardized reading test consisting of 110 items. Joan, age 8-5 in the third grade, gets 42 questions right on the same test. Suppose that the sixth-grade norm is 98 and the third-grade norm is 31 (both norms combine the results of both sexes).

   (a) What is Joan's reference population? _____

   (b) What is Ellen's reference population? _____

   (c) Assuming that the test is a good measure of reading ability, who can read better at this time? _____

   (d) Which one is more likely to be considered a better reader by her own teacher? Why? _____

   _____

   (e) Which one is more likely to be a better reader relative to others in her same grade? _____

5. Suppose that both girls had taken the same test on another day. Label each of the following as either "probable," "doubtful," or "impossible."

   _____ Their scores on another day would have been identical to the scores they actually obtained on the day they took the test

   _____ Joan might have scored higher then Ellen on another day

6. Assume that the norms on this test had been computed on the basis of a large group of students of both sexes from all sections of the country. This group would be referred to as the:

_____ reference population
_____ standardization sample
_____ grade equivalents
_____ none of the above

Answers

1. Mean: 15
    Median: 16
    (frames 16-19)

2. Any or all of the following:
    The score of 90 might be a higher percentage of possible correct answers than the score of 75 (or there might have been more total points to get in the English test, which is saying the same thing).
    The English test might have been more difficult than the arithmetic test.
    Karl's English score might have represented more improvement in terms of his own performance than his arithmetic score.
    The average score in the English test might have been considerably lower than the average score in the arithmetic test.
    (frames 13-16)

3. Raw score
    (frames 13-14)

4. (a) Joan's reference population: students in the sixth grade
    (b) Ellen's reference population: students in the third grade
         (You should not have specified sex because the norms were based on combined results of both sexes. Also, both students in the example are girls anyway, so sex differences, if any, are not important.)
    (c) Ellen, whose score is considerably higher than Joan's, can undoubtedly read better. Another way to look at the question is: if you gave them a sixth-grade book, who would read it better?
    (d) Joan's own teacher is likely to consider her a "good reader," since her test score (which was assumed to reflect reading ability) is higher than the average in her grade level. Ellen's own teacher may well consider Ellen to be below average in reading, since her score was below her grade norm.
    (e) Joan. This is essentially a rephrasing of the preceding question.
    (frames 22-32)

5.   Both statements are <u>doubtful</u>. Either or both of the girls might have been in a different mood, had more or less sleep the night before, eaten a better or worse breakfast, etc. The chances are strong that one or both of them would have obtained a somewhat different result, but it is doubtful that the difference could be as great as 42 points out of 110. The discussion of "measurement error" in frames 1-5 would suggest that the effects are not <u>that</u> large.

6.   Standardization sample
      (frames 21-22)

CHAPTER TWO

Percentile Ranks and Standard Scores

1.   The most common method of describing how a person stands in relation to a reference population is the <u>percentile rank.</u> A person's percentile rank indicates the percentage of results that are <u>below</u> his own.

    Suppose that on a certain test, Walter's result is in the 91st percentile. What does this mean?

    _____ He is close to the top--only 9 percent of the persons in the reference population obtained better scores
    _____ He is close to the bottom--only 9 percent of the persons in the reference population obtained worse scores

- -

He is close to the top--only 9 percent of the persons
in the reference population obtained better scores

2.   In Chapter 1 we measured the height of John Williams and obtained a result of 79 inches. From your own knowledge or observation of the heights of 16-year-old American boys, John's height of 79 inches would probably fall in which percentile?

    _____ 1st
    _____ 5th
    _____ 95th
    _____ 99th

    According to the answer you gave, this means that out of every one hundred 16-year-old American boys, how many would be taller than John? _____

- -

99th
1 out of 100

3.   If you answered "1st" or "5th" percentile, you have reversed the definition. The percentile describes the percentage of persons in a given reference population who are <u>below</u> the result in questions (in this case, 79 inches).

If you answered "95th" percentile and "5 out of 100," you probably have the right idea about what a percentile means. You were not given any figures on how heights of 16-year-old boys are actually distributed, so if you think that five our of one hundred 16-year-old American boys actually are 6'7" or over, and you answered 95th percentile on this basis, then you can consider yourself correct.

As we mentioned earlier, if John's reference population were 16-year-old male Watusi, then he would only be about <u>average</u> height--in other words, probably somewhere around the _____ percentile in that reference population.

- -

50th

4.   Although it is intuitively obvious that the 50th percentile is "somewhere around the average," this is not always true--and, in any event, we need to be more exact.

We cannot tell, from inspection of only the raw score, what percentile rank it falls in. To do so we would have to arrange every single score in rank order (as on page 9) and then compute the percentage of scores falling above and below each one. With the large numbers of persons who take standardized tests, this is impractical (even with electronic computers). For the same reason it is difficult to compute the median. Instead, when dealing with large numbers of persons, we usually compare each score with the other kind of average, which, in review, is known as the _____.

- -

mean

5.   The extent to which a given score is different from the mean is the single most important concept in the statistical interpretation of tests. It is the basis for IQ scores, College Board scores, and indeed the scores of almost every standardized test.

Suppose the mean score of all third-grade boys on an arithmetic achievement test is 70. Arthur's score is 75. Is this to be considered "average," "roughly average," "above average," or "significantly above average"? What percentile would it represent? We can't answer these questions just from the numbers. We need to know how all the scores on the test are <u>distributed,</u> and the extent to which they tend to vary from the average.

If you have previously worked with the "normal curve," you may skip right now to frame 11. If you are also familiar with the concept of standard deviation you can skip to frame 16. Otherwise go on to the next frame.

(<u>No answer necessary</u>.)

6.   Earlier, when you concluded that 16-year-old John Williams was "very tall" and probably in the 99th percentile in terms of height, you could only have done so because you were familiar with the <u>distribution</u> of heights in this reference population. You knew the following facts:

(1) The mean height of boys this age is about 68 inches. This is also the most common height and the median height.

(2) Most boys will be within a few inches of the mean height--say, 3 or 4--in either direction.

(3) The farther any given height is from the mean (in either direction), the less likely that height is to occur in the population.

These facts can be portrayed diagrammatically, as in the accompanying diagram. Which letter in the diagram indicates statement 1? (A/B/C) Which indicates statement 2? _____ Statement 3? _____

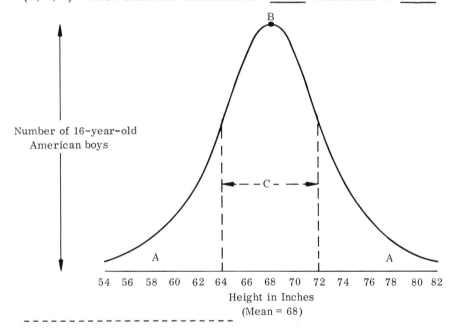

Number of 16-year-old American boys

54 56 58 60 62 64 66 68 70 72 74 76 78 80 82

Height in Inches
(Mean = 68)

- -

Statement 1: B
Statement 2: C
Statement 3: A

7.   The preceding diagram is an example of the well-known "bell-shaped" curve, referred to technically as the <u>normal</u> <u>distribution.</u>" The word "normal" has a mathematical definition which we need not discuss. A commonsense way of thinking about this curve is that it shows how abilities are usually, or "normally," distributed in any given population--that is, relatively few persons at either extreme, with most people located at or near the mean.

Whether we are talking about height, intelligence, arithmetic achievement, or anything else that can be measured, we find that this is either actually the case or is a convenient assumption to make.

Exhibit 2 (page 127) shows the same distribution of heights. The area under the curve represents everybody in the reference population. If we want to know the relative standing of any given individual, we locate his result under the curve. For example, in Exhibit 2, the arrow indicates John's height of 79 inches.

Which letter indicates the number of persons who are taller than John? (A/B/C)

_____   area A
_____   area B
_____   line C

Which letter represents the number of persons who are John's height? _____
Which letter represents the persons who are shorter than John? _____

- -

A   (taller than John)
C   (John's height)
B   (shorter than John)

8.   Simply by comparing area A with the total area under the curve, then, we arrive at the same conclusion that we estimated earlier-- that John is in the 99th percentile in regard to height. This is only approximate, however. To be certain of this we would have to know the exact shape of the distribution, and we would have to know exactly how to measure area under a curve. In practice this is not feasible. Instead, we use mathematics rather than eyesight. Therefore all visual examples in this book are to be taken as only approximations for illustrative purposes.

We began this discussion in frame 5 with an example in which Arthur scored 75 on a test in which the mean score in his reference population was 70. The interpretation of his score depends on the distribution of all scores. We can assume that the scores are distributed in the bell-shaped or "normal" pattern (and will do so throughout, unless exceptions are specifically noted). But this still leaves many possibilities. Exhibit 3 (page 128) shows two possible distributions (A and B). Both are normal, with a mean of 70.

In Exhibit 3-A, the shaded portion is approximately 15 percent of the total area of the curve. This would indicate that a score of 75 is in the _____ percentile.

- -

85th (only 15 percent of the scores are higher)

9.   Now focus on Exhibit 3-B. Approximately what percentage of the total area would the shaded portion represent?

_____ 10 percent
_____ 30 percent
_____ 50 percent

Given your own answer, what percentile would this represent?

_ _

30 percent
70th percentile

10.   In both cases we were focusing on a five-point deviation from the mean. In the two distributions the mean itself was the same (70), but the significance of the five-point deviation from the mean was quite different. The reason is that the <u>variability</u> of the two distributions was different.
       This is not an easy concept because ultimately it depends on mathematics rather than visualization. However, we can informally define variability in several different ways. All of the following statements have the same meaning:

    (1)   The curve is less sharply peaked, indicating
          a greater dispersion of scores.
    (2)   The distribution is spread out more.
    (3)   A given score picked at random is more likely
          to be farther away from the mean.
    (4)   There is greater variability within the population
          distribution.

       Comparing the two distributions in Exhibit 3, to which of them do all these statements apply? (A/B)

_ _

B

11.   All we have at this point is the rather hazy notion that interpretation of scores depends on how they tend to vary. But how do we measure "variability"? Once we have answered this question it will be easier to see how variability relates to the interpretation of scores.
       If you are familiar with the concept of <u>standard deviation</u>, you may skip now to frame 16.

(<u>No answer necessary</u>.)

12.   The standard deviation measures the extent to which scores tend
to deviate from the mean. There is no other way to define the standard deviation except by actually computing it and working with it.
Suppose we have five scores, as follows:

Scores	Difference between each score and the mean (7)
10	3
5	-2
6	-1
11	___
3	___

The total of the scores is 35, so the mean is 7 in this example.
In column 2, we list each deviation from the mean, found by subtracting the mean, 7, from each score. Complete column 2 for the last
two scores.

- -

(Compare your answer with column 2 below.)

13.   Column 2 now represents the deviations from the mean. For
reasons we need not go into, these deviations are <u>squared</u> in order to
compute the standard deviation. The result in column 3 will always
be a positive number, since a minus number squared becomes a positive number. We then add the total squared deviations. For practice,
fill in the last two entries in column 3 and total the column.

(Column 1)	(Column 2)	(Column 3)
	Difference between each score and the mean (7)	Square of column 2
Score		
10	3	9
5	-2	4
6	-1	1
11	4	___
3	-4	___

- -

(Column 3)

9
4
1
16
16
___
46

14.   The result, 46 in this example, is the sum of the squared deviations from the mean. We divide this sum by n - 1, where n is the number of scores we are dealing with (in this case five). <u>Why</u> we divide by n - 1 rather than n is another theoretical question that we need not discuss. In fact, it is difficult to say "why" we do any of these computations. All we can say is that the result proves to be useful, and this fact we <u>will</u> be able to demonstrate.

Dividing the sum of the squared deviations by n - 1 gives us, in this example, a result of 11.5 (46 ÷ 4). We then take the square root of this figure, which turns out to be 3.4. This is the standard deviation for this set of scores. Again, we will skip the question of "why" the square root is taken.

In this example, the scores were 10, 5, 6, 11, and 3. The mean was 7. Suppose the scores had been the following: 4, 6, 7, 8, 10. The mean once again is 7. In the second set, would you expect the standard deviation to be smaller or larger? _____

Briefly explain why you made your choice.

_____

- -

smaller
There seems to be less deviation from the mean of 7 <u>or</u> the scores don't vary as much (or similar answer).

15.   We can verify this by computing the standard deviation for the second set. The computations are given below. The result is a standard deviation of 2.2, as opposed to 3.4 in the first example.

There is little point in studying this example in itself, since in practice there are better ways to compute the standard deviation. The interesting point is to compare columns 2 and 3 with the corresponding columns in frame 13 to see how the standard deviation is influenced by each individual deviation from the mean.

Score	Deviation from mean	Squared deviation
4	-3	9
6	-1	1
7	0	0
8	1	1
10	3	9
35		20 = sum of squared deviation

mean = 7

$20 ÷ (n - 1) = 20 ÷ 4 = 5$

$\sqrt{5} = 2.2$ = standard deviation

(<u>No answer necessary.</u>)

16.   Now turn once again to Exhibit 3 (page 128) where we have shown two possible distributions of scores on a test. (If you originally skipped to this point then you have not yet seen Exhibit 3, but you still should be able to answer the question.)

In which of the two do we find more scores that are within a few points of the mean? (A/B)

The one you answered should therefore have a (HIGHER/LOWER) standard deviation than the other one. In other words, there is (MORE/LESS) variability in that distribution.

- -

A
LOWER
LESS (If you were incorrect on any, and skipped originally, go back to frame 5, page 21.)

17.   You can answer the following questions by referring to the accompanying diagrams or by reviewing the points that were made in frames 8-10.

In diagram A, the low-variability distribution, the score of 75 turned out to be in the _____ percentile. In diagram B, the high-variability distribution, the same score turned out to be in the _____ percentile.

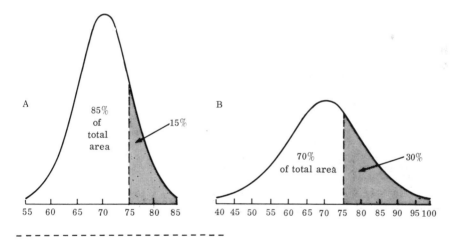

- -

85th
70th

18.   What this shows is that the significance of any given score depends on the variability--that is, the standard deviation--of all scores. Therefore, instead of talking about a certain score as being so many points away from the mean, we want to describe it in terms of how many standard deviations it is from the mean.

Suppose the mean of a distribution of scores is 50, and the standard deviation is 10. A score of 60 would be one SD (standard deviation) away from the mean. A score of 70 would be _____ SD's away from the mean; a score of 75 would be _____ SD's away.

- - - - - - - - - - - - - - - - - - - -

2.0
2.5
(In all future examples of the standard deviation, take the result to one decimal point as shown above.)

19.   If the score is below the mean, the same calculation is made, but with a minus sign. For example, if the mean is 50, the standard deviation is 8, and Peggy's score is 42, then her score is -1.0 SD's from the mean. If Tony's score is 34, his score differs from the mean by _____ SD's.

- -

-2.0 (The minus sign is necessary to indicate that the score was 2.0 SD's below the mean.)

20.   It is known that in any normal distribution, 68 percent of all scores will be between -1.0 and +1.0 standard deviations from the mean. This is shown in the following diagram.

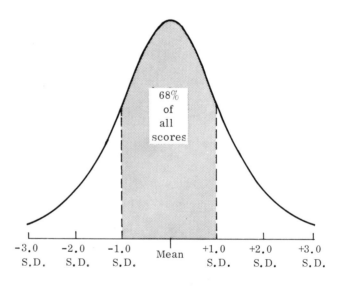

The total area under the curve always represents the entire reference population--in other words, 100 percent. The shaded area represents the proportion who score between -1.0 and +1.0 standard deviations from the mean. If the mean is 70, and the standard deviation is 10, then 68 percent of all scores on this test will be between _____ and _____.

- - - - - - - - - - - - - - - - - - - -

60 and 80

21.   Let us see how this is applied to practical examples.
    The mean of a normal distribution of test scores is 84, with a standard deviation of 6. Joan's score is 90. What percentile does this represent? We will see that this can be answered simply by looking it up in a table. First we'll go over the reasoning that underlies the use of the table.

     (1) From the foregoing facts, we know that Joan's score is _____ SD's from the mean.

- - - - - - - - - - - - - - - - - - - -

+1.0

22.   (2) Given this information, we can locate Joan's score in the normal distribution of all scores, as shown below.
     (3) It is known that 68 percent of all scores fall between -1.0 and +1.0 SD's from the mean.
     (4) The scores that are <u>above</u> the mean but <u>less</u> than +1.0 SD's away from the mean represent _____ of the entire population. (68 or 34 percent?) This is indicated by shaded area _____. (B, C, or B+C?)

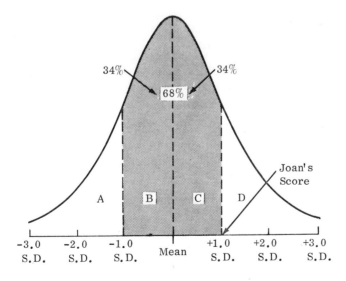

----

34 percent
C

23.   Joan's score is better than these 34 percent in area C of the diagram. In addition, she has done better than all of those whose scores
are below the mean. This accounts for another _____
(34 or 50 percent?) of the entire reference population, as indicated by
area (A/B/A+B) in the preceding diagram.

----

50 percent
A+B

24.   Joan's score, then, exceeds 84 percent of all scores. In review,
this would place her in the _____ percentile. (84th or 16th?)

84th

25.   Obviously this procedure would be of limited value if we could
apply it only to scores that were exactly 1 standard deviation away
from the mean. The formula for the normal distribution enables us
to derive the percentile ranking corresponding to <u>any</u> number of standard deviations. This is shown in Exhibit 4 (page 129). According to
this table (Exhibit 4), a score of 1.4 standard deviations <u>higher</u> than
the mean is in the 92nd percentile. (Notice that we have rounded 91.9
up to the nearest whole number. In all examples using this table,
round <u>up</u> if the decimal is .5 or higher; round <u>down</u> if it is .4 or lower.)
        Using the table as described above, we see that a score of 0.9
standard deviations <u>lower</u> than the mean (as indicated by the minus
signs) is in the _____ percentile.

18th (In Exhibit 4, next to -0.9, we see 18.4 which is rounded down
to 18.)

26.   The number of standard deviations away from the mean--such as
+1.4 or -0.9 in the preceding examples--is the individual's <u>standard
score</u>. It is also known as his "z" score, z being the symbol for number of standard deviations away from the mean.
        Virtually 100 percent of all scores in a normal distribution fall
within <u>three</u> standard deviations from the mean (in both directions).
Thus the highest z score is +3.0, the average z score is 0, and the
lowest z score is _____.

-3.0 (As we will see later, it is possible for some scores to be more than +3.0 or -3.0 standard deviations away from the mean, but for the time being we are limiting ourselves to z values found in the table in Exhibit 4.)

27.   The advantage of a standard score, as the word "standard" implies, is that it always has the same meaning.

In Exhibit 5 (page 130) we show several different normal distributions with different means and standard deviations. In all cases, a z score of, say, +0.3 means that 38 percent of all scores ranked above it. Thus a z score of +0.3 always corresponds to the _____ percentile. (If you're not certain of your answer, you may verify it using Exhibit 4.)

62nd

28.   To arrive at the preceding answer, which of the following did you need to know?

        _____ the subject matter of the test
        _____ the kind of test (written, oral, etc.)
        _____ the length of the test
        _____ all of the above
        _____ none of the above

----

none of the above

29.   Any given percentile rank, such as the 94th, also has the same meaning no matter what kind of test we are concerned with. In fact, the only use that we are going to make of z scores in this book is to convert them to percentiles. The question may arise, then, as to why we use z scores at all in addition to percentiles.

The answer is that certain mathematical operations can be performed with z scores that cannot be performed with percentiles. For example, z scores can be averaged while percentiles cannot. For a discussion of the various uses of z scores and percentiles, and the mathematical assumptions that underlie them, see Lyman, pp. 97-107, and Thorndike and Hagen, pp. 223-224, cited in the Suggestions for Additional Reading.

(No answer necessary.)

30.   You will probably never have to compute z scores regularly in practice. However, you may want to compute the z score of a particular individual on a particular test. In addition, a knowledge of how z scores are computed may make some of the preceding material more understandable, and will also help you understand the interpretation of IQ scores, College Board scores, and a few other well-known scores that are patterned on the normal distribution.

    The formula for a z score is:

$$z = \frac{X - \overline{X}}{s}$$

in which the letter X refers to the individual raw score, the symbol $\overline{X}$ (pronounced X-bar) always refers to the mean, and the letter s refers to the standard deviation.

    Example 1: Joan's score is 70. The mean is 50 and the standard deviation is 10. Substituting in the formula, Joan's z score is found to be:

$$z = \frac{70 - 50}{10} = \frac{20}{10} = 2.0$$

Is this +2.0 or −2.0? _____
Why? _____

- -

plus
Her score was <u>above</u> the mean (<u>or</u> X − $\overline{X}$ was positive).
(This example is identical to the first question you did mentally in frame 18. You might want to check back to that frame.)

31.   Example 2: Carl scores 37 on a standardized arithmetic test. The mean is 40 and the standard deviation is 5. Applying the z-score formula,

$$z = \frac{37 - 40}{5} = \underline{\hspace{2cm}}$$

and Carl's z score is _____.

- -

$$z = \frac{-3}{5} = -0.6$$

32.   Example 3: The mean on a certain test is 60 and the standard deviation is 8.4. Amy's score is 70. Using the formula in frame 30, compute Amy's z score: _____.

    From Exhibit 4 (page 129), what percentile would this be equivalent to? _____

- -

$$z = \frac{(70 - 60)}{8.4} = 1.2$$

89th percentile (88.5 rounded up to 89)

(Note: Here is the best place to take a break in this chapter.)

33.   The normal distribution and the standard-score concept are the
basis for interpreting the scores of the College Board examinations,
the Stanford-Binet intelligence test, and many other tests in wide use.
       The College Board examinations, as you may recall from your
own experience, occur in two parts. The morning portion consists of
the Scholastic Aptitude Test, hereafter referred to as the SAT. This
is actually two tests, one verbal and one mathematical. The afternoon
portion consists of three achievement tests in high-school subjects
selected by the student--for example, a foreign language, a science,
and so on. Since all of these tests use the same scoring system, the
following discussion applies to any CEEB (College Entrance Examination Board) examination.
       The mean score on a CEEB exam is 500. The standard deviation
is 100. The distribution of scores is normal.
       In review, in a normal distribution, the lowest z score, corre-
sponding to 3 SD's below the mean, is _____, and the highest z score
is _____.

- -

-3.0 and +3.0

34.   Given this fact, and the fact that the mean CEEB score is 500 and
the standard deviation is 100, the lowest score has to be -3.0 SD's
away from the mean and the highest score +3.0 SD's away, as indicated in the following diagram. What numbers should be placed next to
the arrows? Enter them in the diagram.

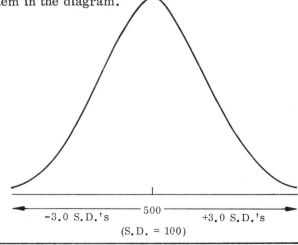

-3.0 S.D.'s   500   +3.0 S.D.'s

(S.D. = 100)

----

200 and 800

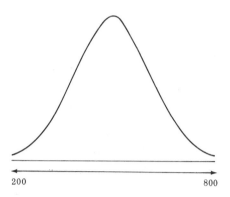

200   800

35.   You probably knew already that this was the range of College
Board scores. Now you know why. These numbers do <u>not</u> represent
the actual number of questions answered correctly. Rather, they correspond to whatever actual number of correct answers would result in
z scores of –3.0 and +3.0.
       It is not important to understand how the original raw scores are
transformed to the artificial numbers of 200, 800, and anything in between. What is important is to understand the meaning of any given
score in terms of the other scores in the reference population.
       Which of the following statements is (or are) correct regarding a
score of 800 on a College Board test?

_____ It is the highest score anyone can obtain.
_____ It means that 800 questions were answered
        correctly.
_____ It places the person in the 100th percentile.
_____ It means that the person scored 3 standard
        deviations above the mean.

- -

It is the highest score anyone can obtain.
It places the person in the 100th percentile.
It means that the person scored 3 standard
deviations above the mean.

36.   Suppose that Roberta scores 630 on the verbal section of the morning examination. How do we find out the corresponding percentile
rank?
        As a first step, let's visualize it. The following diagram shows
the distribution of scores. Roberta's score of 630 is indicated by the
dotted line. Estimate the percentage of total curve area to the right
of this score. _____

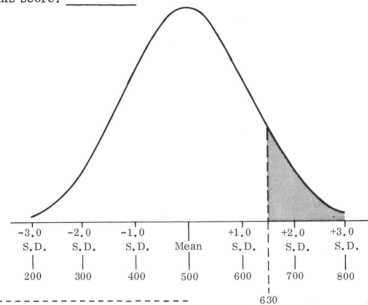

The correct answer, which you have no way of knowing at this point,
is 10 percent. If you guessed anywhere between 5 and 20 percent, you
have the right idea.

37.   Assuming that the shaded portion in the foregoing diagram actually
does represent 10 percent, what percentile rank would this correspond
to? _____

- -

90th
(10 percent of the scores are better than 630, so 90 percent are lower.
The percentile rank indicates the percentage of scores ranking below
a given score.)

38.   The visualization method, of course, is only approximate. To
determine the percentile rank mathematically, first convert the score
(630 in this example) into a z score.
        The mean and standard deviation are 500 and 100, respectively.
Given this information and the formula in frame 30, 630 corresponds
to a z score of _____.

+1.3, as follows:

$$z = \frac{630 - 500}{100} = \frac{130}{100} = +1.3$$

39.   From Exhibit 4 (page 129), a z score of +1.3 corresponds to the _____ percentile.

90th

40.   That's all there is to it. In review, given a score that is known to be based on the normal distribution:

(1) Locate the score in the normal distribution and guess visually what the percentile will be (using the diagram as in frame 36). This helps to guard against a gross error that might result from incorrect computations or from forgetting a plus or minus sign.

(2) Use the formula ($z = \frac{X - \overline{X}}{s}$) to compute the z score. (For any CEEB score, the mean is 500 and the standard deviation is 100.)

(3) Look up the equivalent percentile ranking in Exhibit 4 (page 129).

Suppose now that on the mathematics section of the test, Roberta's score is 530. What percentile rank does this represent?

Guess: _____
z score: _____
Percentile rank: _____

----

(1) If you made a rough guess, based on the normal curve area, it should have been somewhere in the 50's or 60's.

(2) The computation of the z score is:

$$z = \frac{X - \overline{X}}{s} = \frac{530 - 500}{100} = \frac{30}{100} = +0.3$$

(3) This is shown in Exhibit 4 to be equivalent to the 62nd percentile.

41.   We now have the following results for Roberta:

SCHOLASTIC APTITUDE TEST
Roberta Blank

	Score	z	Percentile Rank
Verbal	630	+1.3	90
Mathematical	530	+0.3	62
Average	580	+0.8 (average of +1.3 and +0.3)	

The number 580 represents Roberta's score on the SAT (combining verbal and mathematical). This should correspond to an overall z score of +0.8, as shown above. Let's check to see if z scores can be averaged in this manner. Use the formula to compute the z-score equivalent of a CEEB score of 580.

- -

$$z = \frac{580 - 500}{100} = \frac{80}{100} = +0.8$$

42. Thus we see that z scores can be averaged to get the same result as if we had averaged the scores from which the z units were derived. However, the percentiles cannot be averaged. If we were to average the two percentile ranks, 90 and 62, the result would be

$$\frac{90 + 62}{2} = 76$$

Does a z score of +0.8, Roberta's average for the two parts of the test, actually correspond to the 76th percentile? (YES/NO) Look it up in Exhibit 4.

- -

NO

43. We see from Exhibit 4 that a z score of +0.8 is equal to the 79th percentile, not the 76th percentile. This example shows that z scores (CAN/CANNOT) be averaged and that percentiles (CAN/CANNOT) be averaged.

- -

z scores CAN
percentiles CANNOT

44. The important thing to remember about any score--raw score, standard score, percentile rank, or anything else--is that it tells us something about the individual only in comparison to a specified _____
_____. (If you do not recall the answer immediately, think of how we concluded that 16-year-old John is actually "very tall.")

----

reference population

45.   Suppose that Roberta, with the aid of her high-school guidance
counselor, is deciding whether or not to apply to Radnoke College--a
(fictitious) women's college that ranks academically at the very top.
       If we are estimating her chances of being admitted (and ignoring,
for purposes of illustration, other factors besides College Board
scores), what reference population are we interested in?

        _____ all high-school seniors
        _____ all persons applying to Radnoke
        _____ all female high-school seniors of Roberta's age

----

all persons applying to Radnoke

46.   The percentile computations that we made for Roberta were based
on a normal distribution with mean of 500, standard deviation of 100,
and range of 200 to 800 (as shown in the diagram in frame 36). Is it
likely that the scores of the reference population, "all persons applying to Radnoke," will be distributed around the same mean of 500?
(YES/NO)
       If your answer is NO, would the mean probably be lower or high-
er? _____

NO
higher

47.   It could well be that the scores of applicants to Radnoke will be
distributed as shown in the smaller curve below. Roberta's average
SAT score (combining verbal and mathematical) of 580 was shown to
be in the 79th percentile of the general population of high-school seniors. The same score in the narrower Radnoke distribution, however,
is equivalent (based on your own visual guess) to about the _____ percentile. (Focus only on the smaller curve in answering this question.)

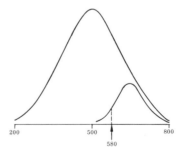

- -

It's obviously well below the 50th percentile, probably below the 25th. Without knowing the mean and standard deviation of the smaller distribution, there's no actual "correct answer."

48.   This does not necessarily mean that the counselor should advise Roberta not to apply to Radnoke. The point of the foregoing example is that a percentile has meaning only when considered as part of a distribution within a given reference population. The 79th percentile in the general population of high-school seniors is of much less significance than the particular population you are interested in.

Incidentally, in an actual counseling situation, the best source of information about qualifications for a particular college is the college itself. Most institutions of higher learning have information leaflets designed for high-school guidance offices, describing the make-up of their student body not only in terms of College Board scores, but also in terms of grade-point averages and other characteristics that influence admissions policies.

(No answer necessary.)

49.   In this chapter we have been using "z score" and "standard score" interchangeably. Often, however, the term "standard score" refers to "T scores," which are simply z scores multiplied by 10 with 50 added. Thus a z score of 1.4 is identical to a T score of (1.4 x 10) + 50, or 64.

If you are interested primarily in an overview of test interpretation, rather than in practical applications, there is no need to be involved with T scores. However, if your work involves standardized tests of educational achievement, you should be familiar with them, since they are very widely used. T scores are discussed in the Appendix (page 142). Whether or not you choose to read the material on T scores, go on with the rest of the book first.

The following test concludes this chapter. In Chapter 3 we will discuss the statistical interpretation of IQ scores.

(No answer necessary.)

TEST FOR CHAPTER 2

For some of the following questions, you may need to refer to the z-score formula on page 32 and the table of percentile ranks on page 129.

1. Tom scores in the 85th percentile. This means that his score is better than _____ of all scores in the reference population. (85 or 15 percent?)

2. In the normal-distribution diagram at the right, the lowest score is at point A and the highest at point H. Which point would be equivalent to about the 20th percentile? _____

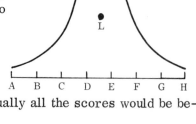

3. The mean of a certain test is 140 and the standard deviation is 30. Assuming that the scores of the test are distributed normally (in the bell-shaped pattern), virtually all the scores would be between:

   (a) 110 and 170
   (b) 80 and 200
   (c) 50 and 230
   (d) no way of telling from the information given

4. Arnold's z score is 1.5. You want to find his percentile rank. In order to use the table you would have to know:

   (a) the mean score
   (b) the standard deviation
   (c) whether the z score was positive or negative (+ or -)
   (d) all of the above
   (e) none of the above

5. Willa's score on a test is 80. The mean is 60 and the standard deviation is 20. What percentile is she in? _____

6. All College Board scores have a mean of 500 and a standard deviation of 100. The lowest score is _____ and the highest is _____. (If you don't recall, you can compute it, given the above information and the fact that all scores on this test are within 3 standard deviations of the mean.)

7. Harold's results on the Scholastic Aptitude Test are as follows:

	Score	Percentile Rank
Verbal	570	_____
Mathematical	490	_____

Guess the percentile rank corresponding to these two scores. (If necessary, look at the diagram in frame 34, page 33.) Compute the percentile ranks (X = 500; SD = 100).

8. The average of the two scores in the above question is 530. How would you determine Harold's result on the combined SAT (verbal and mathematical)?

  (a) Change 530 into a z score of +0.3 and locate the corresponding percentile rank in the table.
  (b) The same, but +0.3 is not the correct figure.
  (c) Neither--simply average the two percentile ranks computed in question 7.

Answers

1. 85 percent (frames 1-3)
2. Point C, as shown in the shaded diagram at the right. If you guessed point B, you probably had the right idea. (frames 7-9)

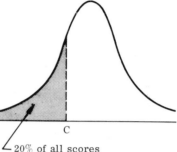
C
20% of all scores

3. (c): 50 and 230 (3 standard deviations, or 90 points, away from the mean in both directions) (frames 26, 33-34)
4. (c): whether the z score was positive or negative (+ or -) (frames 26-29)
5. 84th percentile (Her score is 1 standard deviation away from the mean, so her z score is +1.0. The percentile rank is found in Exhibit 4, or you might have remembered that +1.0 is equivalent to the 84th percentile.) (frames 23-24)
6. 200 and 800 (frames 33-34)
7. (a) Your guess for the verbal percentile rank should have been somewhere above the 60th and below the 90th percentile; for the mathematical percentile rank, somewhere below the 50th and above the 40th percentile. (These numbers are arbitrary; consider yourself basically correct if you guessed above the 50th on verbal and below the 50th on mathematical.)
   (b)
   Verbal: $z = \dfrac{570 - 500}{100} = +0.7$; percentile rank = 76

   Mathematical: $z = \dfrac{490 - 500}{100} = -0.1$; percentile rank = 46

   (frames 36-40)
8. Change 530 into a z score of +0.3 and locate the corresponding percentile rank in the table. The result (not required in the question) is a percentile rank of 62. (frames 41-42)

CHAPTER THREE

IQ Scores

1.   Modern intelligence testing began with the work of Alfred Binet in France late in the nineteenth century. Binet's procedures were revised and augmented by Lewis M. Terman and his associates at Stanford University; hence the name Stanford-Binet for the test that introduced the term "I.Q." to education and psychology.

    The term has several different meanings. With periods after the letters, "I.Q." stands for "Intelligence Quotient." This terminology is no longer correct, since the quotient method is no longer used. We will discuss it briefly, and then show the correct way--and a few incorrect ways--of using the term and the concept.

(<u>No answer necessary</u>.)

2.   The raw scores of the Stanford-Binet are in terms of a "mental age" such as 80 months (e.g., 6 years and 8 months, abbreviated 6-8). A child who achieves this score, whatever his actual chronological age, has done as well at the various tasks as children in the standardization sample who actually were 80 months of age.

    In some tasks--for example, repeating numbers that are read to him--a child may perform at, say, the 72-month level. In others-- for example, arranging pictures in a logical sequence--he might perform at, say, the 96-month level. His performance on all tasks is combined to yield a single mental age.

    If a child has a mental age of 80 and actually is 80 months old, then, by definition, he is of "average" intelligence. If a child's mental-age score is 80 and he is only, say, 74 months of age chronologically, then he would be (ABOVE/BELOW) average in intelligence.

- -

ABOVE

3.   But as always when comparing a person's score with an average, we have to ask <u>how much</u> above average. Significantly? Mildly? Moderately? Incredibly? And how do we compare the performance of different children with different chronological and mental ages?

Using the old "ratio I.Q." method, the mental age was divided by the chronological age. Thus a child who achieved a score of 80 and was 74 months old would have a ratio I.Q. of 80/74 or 1.08. The mental/chronological ratio was multiplied by 100 purely for convenience, resulting in an Intelligence Quotient of 108 in this example.

In this system what would be the I.Q. of a child of 6-0 who achieved a mental age of 9-0?

> Step 1: Divide mental age (MA) by chronological age (CA):
> $$9/6 = 1.50$$
> Step 2: Multiply by 100: I.Q. = 1.50 x 100 = 150

A child is 66 months of age and achieves a mental-age score of 62. Before doing his ratio I.Q., do you expect the answer to be above 100 or below? _____ Why? _____
What is his I.Q. according to this method? _____

- -

It would have to be below 100 because the child's mental age is less than his chronological age (or he is performing below his age level, or similar answer).
94   (62 ÷ 66 = 0.939 or 0.94; 0.94 x 100 = 94)

4.   The ratio method worked well enough for almost half a century, but it has a few flaws. Since the problems are basically statistical in nature we will only mention them, without going into the technicalities.

    (1) Intelligence does develop with age, as the scoring system presupposes, but not at a uniform rate from year to year.

    (2) The variability of mental-age scores turned out to be different at different chronological ages. As you might expect, variability was greater at very young and older ages (3 and 12, for example) than at intermediate ages. As a result of this fact (and item 1 above), ratio I.Q.'s at different ages are not exactly comparable.

    (3) The ratio method was unique to the Stanford-Binet test. The newer method is based on statistical properties of the normal distribution that are common to many tests.

    (4) Since virtually all basic intelligence skills are developed by the early or middle teens, beyond that time the "mental age" concept is not usable. A 35-year-old and a 24-year-old of equal capabilities would have the same mental-age score, so the quotient method (ratio I.Q.) would not be practical.

This does not mean that ratio I.Q.'s are "invalid." In fact, an I.Q. computed on the old basis represents approximately the same level of intelligence as IQ's computed on the new (post-1960) basis that we will now discuss.

(No answer necessary.)

5.   In 1960 the Stanford-Binet test was revised and updated, and the scoring system was changed from the "ratio I.Q." method to the "deviation IQ" method.

Using the deviation IQ method, the average IQ at any age is still 100. The standard deviation at all ages has been set equal to 16. How this is done, and the logical and statistical basis for doing it, is beyond our scope. When we discussed CEEB scores we stated that the mean is 500 and the standard deviation 100, and then showed how we could work with these figures. We'll do the same for deviation IQ scores. The important thing to remember is that deviation IQ scores are normally distributed with a mean of 100 and standard deviation of 16.

Since we know the mean IQ and the standard deviation, we can transform any individual's Stanford-Binet IQ into a z score and then find the percentile equivalent, exactly as we did with CEEB scores. For example, Tom's IQ, as measured by the Stanford-Binet test, is 108. What percentile does this represent?

Step 1: Convert the score into a z score, using the formula:

$$z = \frac{X - \overline{X}}{s}$$

X, the individual's score, was given as 108. From the information elsewhere in this frame, on the Stanford-Binet $\overline{X}$ = _____ and s = _____.

- -

$\overline{X}$ = 100 (the mean)
s = 16 (the standard deviation)

6.   Substituting in the formula in the preceding frame, what is Tom's z score? _____

From Exhibit 4 (page 129), what percentile does this correspond to? _____

- -

$z = +0.5 \; (z = \frac{108 - 100}{16} = \frac{8}{16} = 0.5)$
69th percentile

7.   As a rough check on our computations, and as a review of earlier material, let's visualize this result in terms of the normal distribution of IQ scores.

In the following diagram, Tom's IQ score of 108 is represented by arrow _____ (C or D?).

What percentage of the area should be to the right of it? _____
What percentage to the left? _____

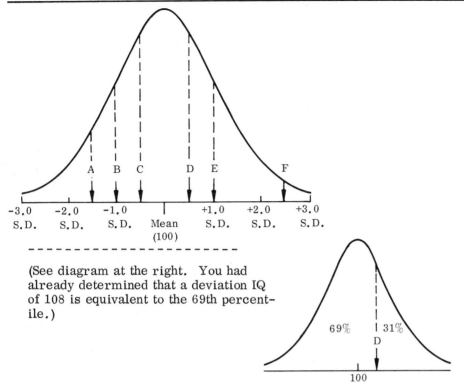

A   B   C   D E   F

-3.0	-2.0	-1.0		+1.0	+2.0	+3.0
S.D.	S.D.	S.D.	Mean	S.D.	S.D.	S.D.
			(100)			

(See diagram at the right. You had already determined that a deviation IQ of 108 is equivalent to the 69th percentile.)

69% | 31%
      D

100

8.   Given that the mean is 100, the choice was easy to make since 108 is above the mean. Arrows E and F were also above the mean, but probably seemed to be too far away to represent 108 on the scale.

As we did in our study of College Board scores, we will use a combination of visual and arithmetical techniques to understand the meaning of "deviation IQ" in terms of the normal distribution. In the following diagram, given that the mean is 100 and the standard deviation is 16, fill in the correct numbers under each arrow. One of them, 84, has been entered to give you a start.

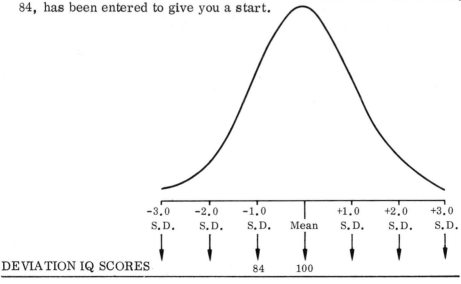

| -3.0 | -2.0 | -1.0 | | +1.0 | +2.0 | +3.0 |
| S.D. | S.D. | S.D. | Mean | S.D. | S.D. | S.D. |

DEVIATION IQ SCORES

84   100

- -

(Correct answer is given in the diagram in Exhibit 6 (page 131). Look at Exhibit 6 and keep a bookmark there.)

9.   Tom's IQ score of 108 is halfway between the mean and $+1.0$ SD; thus it is indicated in Exhibit 6 by the X which corresponds to arrow D in the diagram in frame 7.

The following exercises are identical to those we have already done with CEEB scores, except that now our mean is 100 and SD is 16. In each exercise the "IQ" referred to is a deviation IQ with mean 100 and SD 16. For each IQ given,

1.   locate it on the diagram (Exhibit 6) and make a rough guess as to what percentile it is equivalent to;
2.   convert it into a z score; and
3.   look up the percentile equivalent on Exhibit 4.

Sally's IQ score is 94. What percentile does this represent?

Guess: _____
z score: _____
Percentile from Exhibit 4: _____

- -

$$z = \frac{94 - 100}{16} = \frac{-6}{16} = -0.4$$

Percentile rank: 35th

10.   If your original guess was anywhere between the 25th and 45th percentile, that's close enough. The purpose of the guess, other than to familiarize yourself with the normal distribution, is to serve as a check against a gross error.

The following exercises are simply for practice in working with deviation IQ's. They may be skipped if you got the previous one correct. In each case (or for as many as you care to do), convert the deviation IQ (DIQ) into a z score and a percentile rank (PR). The mean is 100 and the standard deviation 16. (Note that DIQ is an abbreviation for "deviation IQ," as opposed to the "ratio I.Q." discussed earlier.)

		Your guess based on location in normal curve	z score	Percentile rank (PR)
(1)	DIQ			
(1)	112	_____	_____	_____
(2)	88	_____	_____	_____
(3)	78	_____	_____	_____
(4)	132	_____	_____	_____

- -

Answers to Practice Exercises

(1)   z = +0.8; PR = 79th

$$\frac{112 - 100}{16} = \frac{12}{16} = 0.75 = +0.8$$

(2)   z = -0.8; PR = 21st

$$\frac{88 - 100}{16} = \frac{-12}{16} = -0.75 = -0.8$$

(3)   z = -1.4; PR = 8th

$$\frac{78 - 100}{16} = \frac{-22}{16} = -1.4$$

(4)   z = 2.0; PR = 98th

$$\frac{132 - 100}{16} = \frac{32}{16} = +2.0$$

11.   As stated earlier, virtually 100 percent of all scores in a normal distribution fall between -3.0 and +3.0 standard deviations from the mean. Thus virtually 100 percent of all deviation IQ scores would be between _____ at the low end and _____ at the high end.

-   .

52 and 148

12.   If you missed this answer, you can see how it was arrived at by looking once again at Exhibit 6. In that diagram, and all normal curve diagrams, you may have noticed that the ends of the curve do not quite touch the baseline. Actually they extend somewhat beyond the limits of -3.0 and +3.0 standard deviations, and in theory you could get an extreme score an infinite distance away from the mean.
   If you now look at Exhibit 4, you can see that a z score of +3.0 is superior not to exactly 100 percent of all scores, but to _____ percent of all scores. You can also see that _____ percent of all scores are below -3.0 standard deviations from the mean.

- -

99.9 percent
0.1 percent

13.   What this means is that approximately 1 out of 1,000 persons will achieve an IQ score of over 148 or below 52. It's not necessary to remember "1 out of 1,000," since that's only an approximation anyway.

What is important is that there may be some scores that will be above +3.0 or below -3.0 standard deviations from the mean, so you shouldn't think it's a misprint if you run across an IQ score below 52 or above 148.

(No answer necessary.)

14.   The deviation IQ concept was developed originally as a scoring system not for the Stanford-Binet, but for the Wechsler Adult Intelligence Scale (WAIS), the Wechsler Intelligence Scale for Children (WISC), and the Wechsler Preschool and Primary Scale (WPPSI). Since all three Wechsler tests are similar in form and in scoring system, we can simply refer to "the Wechsler" without differentiating among the three.

Like the Stanford-Binet, the Wechsler is designed to be administered to one person at a time by a trained examiner. We will not go into the similarities and differences of these two tests. Most textbooks will discuss them and show some sample items. The one point relevant to our purpose right now is that the standard deviation of the Wechsler IQ is 15, not 16. The mean is 100.

Thus a score of 115 on the Wechsler is equivalent to a z score of _____ and a percentile rank of _____.

As an optional exercise, a Stanford-Binet IQ of 115 is equivalent to a z score of _____ or the _____ percentile.

- -

Wechsler: z = +1.0; PR = 84
Stanford-Binet: z = +0.9; PR = 82

15.   The major advantage of the deviation IQ concept is that, like any standard score, it has the same mathematical interpretation no matter what the test. Thus we can score other intelligence tests on the same basis. (Keep in mind, however, that the Wechsler SD is 15, not 16.)

For example, the Lorge-Thorndike Intelligence Tests and the Otis-Lennon Mental Ability Tests are two widely used tests which are scored objectively and can be administered to a group, unlike the Stanford-Binet and the Wechsler which can be given to only one individual at a time and which require a trained person to administer and score them. A deviation IQ of 132 on these tests has the same statistical meaning as a Stanford-Binet deviation IQ of 132--namely, that the individual (in this example) has scored _____ standard deviations (ABOVE/BELOW) the mean of his reference population.

- -

+2.0
ABOVE
(In this case you could have omitted the plus sign since you specified "above.")

16.   It is assumed that a person who scores a given number of SD's away from the mean on one intelligence test will probably score in the same range on any other intelligence test; thus 132 is the best guess as to what a person would score on the Stanford-Binet. Of course this assumption, however commonsensical it appears, cannot be left as an assumption. It must be supported by statistical sampling data and by analyses of the tests themselves to indicate that they are, in fact, measuring essentially the same thing.

If IQ scores on different tests are to be comparable, the reference populations as well as the tests themselves must be comparable. In general, unless the manual for a particular test states otherwise, you can assume the following:

(1)   An IQ score is based on a comparison to other persons of the same age (usually to the nearest month).

(2)   This age-based reference population is national, rather than local, regional, or international.

(3)   The IQ score is a deviation IQ rather than a ratio I.Q. This means that it is calculated by which of the following methods?

_____   computing the number of z units by which the person's score differs from the mean of his reference population

_____   dividing mental age by chronological age and multiplying by 100

- - - - - - - - - - - - - - - - - - - -

Computing the number of z units by which the person's
score differs from the mean of his reference population

17.   For any intelligence test that reports a score in the form of an IQ number, you can also assume that the mean IQ score at an age level is 100 and that (with one exception) the standard deviation is the same as in the Stanford-Binet. This number is worth remembering, along with a few others we have discussed. What are the means and standard deviations of each of the following? The first answer has been entered to give you a start.

	Mean	Standard Deviation
(1) Stanford-Binet	100	_____
(2) Wechsler IQ	___	_____
(3) All "deviation IQ's" except Wechsler	___	_____
(4) Scholastic Aptitude Test (morning CEEB examination)	___	_____
(5) All other CEEB examinations	___	_____

- -

(1)	100	16
(2)	100	15
(3)	100	16
(4)	500	100
(5)	500	100

18.   Exhibit 7 (page 132) shows a typical reporting form for a widely used group-administered intelligence test. Keep a bookmark at Exhibit 7 since we will be working with it for several frames.

Exhibit 7 contains the kind of data that persons involved in standardized tests are always working with. (The school and pupils are fictitious, and some information that is not relevant to our discussion has been omitted from the table.)

This particular test is in two parts: verbal and nonverbal. The verbal portion measures verbal reasoning ability, vocabulary, verbal classification, sentence completion, arithmetic reasoning, and verbal analogy. The nonverbal portion consists of pictorial classification, pictorial analogy, and numerical relationships.

Since standard scores can be averaged, deviation IQ's can also be averaged. This is what has been done in this test, and what is usually done with most two-part (e.g., verbal and nonverbal) intelligence tests.

For example, in the last column you see that Lisa Andrews' "total IQ" is 106. What other numbers in the table were used to compute this figure? _____

- -

Lisa's verbal IQ = 109; nonverbal IQ = 103; average of the two = 106. (Since other numbers on this table happen to be similar, make sure you are looking only at the IQ numbers to the right of the "raw score" columns in the "Lisa Andrews" row.)

19.   Not all intelligence tests yield a total IQ that is the result of averaging two components, but all do consist of several different tasks measuring different kinds of skills. Each test is different in this regard, but in general the verbal IQ usually consists of much more than linguistic skills. It also includes arithmetical skills, logic, knowledge of factual information, and sometimes other components as well. (Perhaps "intellectual" would be a better way to think of it than "verbal.)

The perception of spatial relationships, manipulation of blocks, or other tasks requiring visualization and/or dexterity are examples of nonverbal skills.

Given the above, which of the following kinds of questions would you expect to find on the verbal (as opposed to nonverbal) section of an intelligence test?

_____ Problems requiring arithmetical operations
_____ Arranging pictures in a logical sequence
_____ Predicting whether a pair of jigsaw-puzzle
      pieces would fit together
_____ Giving a word that is the opposite of a named word

- -

All but "predicting whether a pair of jigsaw-puzzle pieces would fit together" (If you did not check the three others, reread the first paragraph of frame 19.)

20.   It is often important to know how the different parts of the test-- verbal and nonverbal--contribute to the total IQ. For example, consider the student "Elin Carlson" in Exhibit 7. Her total IQ of 116 is exactly _____ SD's above the mean. This would place her in the _____ percentile. (Note: These answers are not to be found from Exhibit 7 itself.)

- -

1 SD (+1.0)
84th percentile (from Exhibit 4)

21.   From this we might expect that Elin's schoolwork in general would be superior. Suppose, however, that her teacher, Mr. Green, knows that this is not the case. Let's assume that she is in no serious trouble, but that her schoolwork is only fair.
     According to the authors of this particular test (see Thorndike and Hagen, 1969, p. 297) and according to virtually all the literature on the subject as well as what you would expect from common sense, good schoolwork is more likely to be associated with:

_____ primarily verbal intelligence
_____ primarily nonverbal intelligence
_____ both equally

- -

primarily verbal intelligence

22.   Looking up Elin's scores, we discover that her verbal IQ score turns out to be 105; her nonverbal IQ score, 127. How significant a difference is this? The best way to picture it is in regard to the normal distribution. Compared with all children age 15 years and 5 months, Elin's position corresponds to those indicated by the X in each diagram.

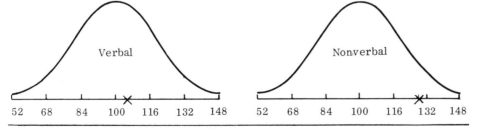

Verbal							Nonverbal					
52	68	84	100	116	132	148	52	68	84	100	116	132	148

From inspection of the diagrams, guess the percentile ranks equivalent to these two scores. Then find the percentile ranks by computation, as in previous exercises.

- -

Verbal: $z = \dfrac{105 - 100}{16} = +0.3$; PR (from Exhibit 4) = 62nd

Nonverbal: $z = \dfrac{127 - 100}{16} = 1.7$; PR = 96th

23. Before going any further with this analysis, we should point out that this case is not typical. In general, verbal IQ and nonverbal IQ are highly correlated. This means that a person who scores high on one usually scores high on the other.

From this sample of students we can see that Elin's case is indeed unusual. One other student, Linda Jensen, also has a large difference (20 points) between verbal and nonverbal IQ; but both her scores are quite high so the correlation still holds.

For practice in reading this kind of table, which other student in the class has a large discrepancy (18 points) between verbal and nonverbal scores and what are those scores?

_____

_____

- -

Chris Ralston
Verbal IQ = 101; nonverbal IQ = 119

24. Given a difference between two scores, we have to ask two questions. First: Is it statistically significant? It is always possible that the two scores, verbal and nonverbal, happened to differ on this test by chance. Perhaps if the student took the same test again, the difference would be less.

A general rule of thumb is that a difference between two scores of 1 standard deviation or more can be considered statistically significant--that is, as being the result of a genuine difference rather than as just a chance result. Using this rule of thumb, consider the verbal and nonverbal scores of Connie Iverson. The difference amounts to
_____ points. Would you consider this to be statistically significant? (YES/NO) Why, or why not? _____

- -

10 points (95 and 105)
NO
Since the standard deviation is 16 points, according to our rule of thumb we would not conclude that the difference is statistically significant (or similar answer).

25.   Given that the difference is statistically significant, the general
question we have to ask is what the difference actually means.

We began this discussion with a hypothetical example in which
Elin Carlson's schoolwork was not as good as might be expected from
her total IQ of 116 (84th percentile). Examining her scores in more
detail, we found her verbal IQ to be 105 and her nonverbal IQ to be
127. You computed the percentiles corresponding to these scores in
frame 22.

These facts could be interpreted in different ways. We might say
that since Elin's overall score is high (total IQ = 116), her schoolwork to date is not a final indication of what she might be able to do.
We note from the table, however, that Elin is almost 15 1/2, and in
the tenth grade. While tenth-grade performance is certainly not a
"final indication" of her academic potential, that kind of interpretation
would probably be more appropriate for a younger child.

If we considered the two scores separately instead of looking at
the total IQ figure, we might think along different lines. Perhaps
Elin's aptitude for schoolwork is only about average--but her high
nonverbal IQ score might suggest that she has the potential to do well
in a nonacademic setting (e.g., in a career that requires high intelligence but not an advanced academic degree).

Whichever way you look at the data--and there are many other
ways to think about it in addition to those mentioned--interpretation
must be done on a highly tentative basis. The fact is that we simply
don't know enough about Elin. We would want to know what her performance has been in earlier years, what her interests are, what
other test results we have, and many other important facts. The point
is not that the IQ scores themselves will tell us what we need to know
about Elin, but that they may give us a clue as to what other information to look for.

Suppose, then, that as a teacher or parent you know only the total
IQ of a given child--say, 97. You know something about the test itself
and you know that this is a deviation IQ score. What else do you need
to know about this total IQ ?

_____

- - - - - - - - - - - - - - - - - - - -

The separate scores for verbal and nonverbal IQ (or similar answer).

(Note: Here is the best place to take a break in this chapter.)

26.　　To the right of the IQ scores in Exhibit 7, we see grade percentiles for each student. At this level (tenth grade) the chances are that
age percentiles and grade percentiles will be highly similar, and the
statistical meaning of a percentile rank is the same no matter what
kind of reference population we are talking about. Thus, in the following discussion, although we happen to be focusing on the grade percentiles in the table, the points made would apply equally to age percentiles.

　　We see in the table that, for verbal IQ, Lisa Andrews has a grade
percentile rank of 70. State what this means in your own words, as if
you were explaining it to someone (a parent, perhaps) who is not familiar with the concepts discussed in this book.

_____

_____

_____

- -

(Answer is discussed below.)

27.　　The problem here is to do justice to the information without getting too technical. You might start out as follows:

　　"On the verbal portion of this test, Lisa's raw score of 51 was
higher than 70 percent of all tenth graders in the United States; in
other words, she is in the top 30 percent of that reference population."

　　If you wanted to go into more depth--and it wouldn't be a bad idea--
you might mention that of course not all tenth graders in the United
States have actually taken this test. To be technically correct we
should say that the score of 51 would have been in the 70th percentile
of a smaller group (perhaps a few thousand) of students who, some
years back, provided the basis for all the norms data. This group is
known as the _____ sample.

- -

standardization

28.　　Assuming that the standardization sample is representative of the
entire population, we can say that the raw score of 51 is in the 70th
percentile of all tenth graders. Now the parent wants to know if this
means that Lisa is "more intelligent" than 70 percent of all tenth graders. This is a correct interpretation of the percentile rank itself.
However, there are some important qualifications we must make before we can state this as a conclusion. Mention a few:

_____

_____

_____

- -

(Answer is discussed below.)

29.   We have to keep in mind that not everyone has the same conception of what it is to be intelligent, or to be more intelligent than some-
body else. Thus we are talking about "intelligence" <u>as measured by
intelligence tests</u> in general, and this test in particular.
        Another qualification you might make is that the raw score, and
therefore the percentile rank, is subject to some degree of measurement error. Lisa might have done better or worse had she taken the
test on another day, or taken another form of the same test.
        Finally, you should have noticed that the percentile rank of 70
came from the verbal score, not from a total score. The parent might
want to know what "verbal" refers to. Although each test is somewhat
different, which of the following would probably be included in the
"verbal" category in most intelligence tests?

_____ arithmetic exercises
_____ picking one design that does not match the other four
_____ vocabulary questions

- -

arithmetic exercises
vocabulary questions

30.   Turning now to the nonverbal score, we see that Lisa's grade
percentile rank is 54. Can we average this with the verbal percentile
rank, 70, and say that Lisa is in the 62nd percentile on combined
verbal and nonverbal IQ? (YES/NO)

- -

NO
Percentiles cannot be averaged. We have not gone into the mathematical reasons as to <u>why</u> this is the case, but we showed an example of
<u>how</u> it would not work out (see frame 42, page 37).
        If these were age percentiles rather than grade percentiles, the
way to find the total percentile would be to take Lisa's total IQ, 106,
and convert it into a z score and a percentile as we have been doing
all along. We know that 16 is the standard deviation for students of
Lisa's age, or any age. That has been built into any test that uses a
deviation IQ (except for the Wechsler scales, in which the standard
deviation is 15). But this is true only with respect to <u>age</u>, not with
respect to <u>grade</u>.
        We cannot get into differences between age norms and grade norms
more deeply without going into more mathematics than the subject
merits. Just bear in mind the following points, both of which have
been discussed in previous chapters:

(1) Deviation IQ scores, which have a mean of 100 and a standard deviation of 15 or 16, can be automatically translated into age percentiles, not grade percentiles. (The grade percentiles in this table have been computed by some other method.)

(2) No matter what kind of test or what kind of reference population we are concerned with, percentiles cannot be averaged.

31.   Next to the grade percentiles in Exhibit 7, we see age and grade equivalents. For example, the table says that Terry Brown's raw score of 65 on the verbal section is "equivalent" to age 18 years, 6 months. We know that most children who are actually this age would not be in the tenth grade; in fact, if still in school they would probably be freshmen or possibly sophomores in college.

If you were asked the meaning of the 18-6 age equivalent, what would you say (on the basis of our discussion in Chapter 1)?

_____ Those persons in the standardization sample who were this age had an average score of 65 on this portion of the test.

_____ Terry is capable of doing college work right now.

_____ Terry is an unusually mature 15-year-old.

- -

Those persons in the standardization sample who were 18 years and 6 months old had an average score of 65 on this portion of the test. (If you answered any of the others, you might review frames 29-34, pages 13-15.)

32.   As we look down the column we find that no fewer than eight out of 18 children in this class have the identical age equivalent of 18-6. Yet their raw scores were different, ranging from Terry's 65 to Philip Norton's 56. This appears to be an extremely wide range of scores for one age group (18-6) to have averaged. What must have happened is that the standardization sample did not go beyond this age group, or that, beyond the age of 18-6, there simply was no improvement in scores. This is an example of a ceiling.

Age equivalents themselves are misleading, and ceilings make them doubly misleading. If we looked only at the age equivalent, 18-6, we would have to conclude that Philip did as well on the test as Terry. This is not the case, however. We find that Terry's raw score of 65 yields a deviation IQ of 121, a difference of 9 points or more than half a standard deviation greater than Philip's IQ of 112.

What probably happened, then, was that Philip, Terry, and everyone else with this age-equivalent score of 18-6 did well enough on the test to go over the ceiling. This disguises the individual differences among them, which might actually be great.

The "ceiling effect" is shown even more dramatically in the non-verbal section of the table. We find that 12 out of 17 students in this classroom have a nonverbal age-equivalent score of 18-6. Yet it would be most unwise to consider them equal in nonverbal intelligence. As you can verify yourself, the raw scores of these 12 children range from 45 to 61, and the nonverbal deviation IQ scores range from Ronald Gorla's _____ to Linda Jenson's _____ .

- -

115
141 (If you were incorrect you were probably looking at the verbal instead of the nonverbal section.)

33.   We won't spend any time with the "grade equivalent" column except to mention a typographical point which you might want to be aware of on other computerized test-score reports. Look at the grade-equivalent column for the verbal section--118, 121, 108, and so on. These numbers look like IQ numbers, but they are not. You have to insert a decimal point to the left of the last digit. Thus the grade equivalent for Lisa Andrews is not 118, but 11.8--that is, the eighth month of the eleventh grade.
    Notice that there are several grade-equivalent scores of 12.1 (121 in the table, with the decimal point mentally inserted), and that there are no scores higher than this. What does this lead you to suppose?

_____

- -

12.1 is the ceiling <u>or</u>
The standardization sample did not go beyond students in grade 12.1
<u>or</u>
Students beyond 12.1 do not score any higher (<u>or similar answers</u>)

34.   Another point to notice in Exhibit 7 is that the same raw score may result in a different IQ. For example, Larry Dylhoff and Sandra Fox both had a raw score of 45 on the verbal section of the test. Why is Sandra's verbal IQ 103, and Larry's only 102? To answer this question, and virtually any question concerned with the interpretation of standardized test scores, you will never go wrong by asking yourself <u>what is the reference population?</u> In Larry's case the raw score of 45 is being compared with the scores achieved by all children age 15 years and 9 months (15-9). Sandra's score is being compared with the scores achieved by all children age 15-7, as shown in the table.
    Since scores in IQ tests tend to improve as a child gets older (even at this relatively late age), the raw score of the older child, Larry, would have to be slightly (HIGHER/LOWER) than Sandra's in order to result in the same deviation IQ score.

HIGHER

35.   Since their raw scores on the verbal portion of the test were the
same (45, as shown in the table), Larry's verbal deviation IQ turns
out to be very slightly lower than Sandra's. This example was given
only to review the concept of "reference population," and to point out
that the numbers were not misprints. In general, however, it is very
hard to think of anything that could be <u>less</u> significant than a one-point
difference in IQ.

We need the numbers to be able to do certain kinds of statistical
analysis. For most practical purposes, however, it is wise to consider IQ's in terms of <u>ranges</u> rather than individual numbers.

There are two major reasons for this statement. First, it is impossible to say what is actually represented by one IQ point, or indeed
any number of IQ points or points on any kind of test. It is not like an
"inch" that can be seen or a "pound" that can be felt. For this reason,
we have emphasized what scores mean in terms of the normal distribution as a way of visualizing where people stand in relation to the
mean.

Second, if the difference between two IQ's is small, it could well
be a matter of measurement error. As you may recall, "measurement error" refers to:

_____ mistakes made in administering or scoring a test
_____ inevitable differences in results if additional
             measurements are taken

----

inevitable differences in results if additional measurements are taken
(Review frames 3-5, pages 2-3, if you missed this or do not recall
the earlier discussion of "measurement error.")

36.   What this means, as discussed earlier in connection with John
Williams' height, is that 103 is only the best guess we can make as to
Larry's "true" IQ. As we will see in the final chapter, through the
use of a few formulas, we can say there is approximately a 5 percent
chance that if he took the same test again, his verbal IQ score would
turn out to be below 92 or above 114.

Usually, then, IQ's and other test scores are interpreted in terms
of a probable range of values, rather than an absolute value. This
guards against imputing more significance to a single number than is
actually warranted. However, arbitrary range classifications can also
be misleading.

For example, in working with or reading about intelligence tests,
particularly the Stanford-Binet, you are likely to come across the word
"normal" to describe persons in connection with IQ's between 88 and
112 (or possibly 90 and 110); 112 to 124 is often labeled "superior";
124 to 128 "very superior"; and above 148, "genius."

These words, and their counterparts on the lower end of the IQ scale, can be misleading for several reasons.

Let's just consider the label "superior." On the basis of what you have read in this book, which of the following (if any) could justify the use of this word in regard to IQ scores of 112 to 124?

_____ A score in this range is above average, and "superior" can be taken as a synonym for "above average."

_____ A child who scores in this range has qualities that set him apart from most of his peers.

- -

A score in this range is above average, and "superior" can be taken as a synonym for "above average."

37.   This is the only justification for the use of the word "superior." All we know from a table such as Exhibit 7, or from any test result, is the score. We also know the mean and standard deviation for the individual's reference population. Thus we can use the word "super-ior" just as we could use the term "very tall" to apply to a boy who was several inches above average height.

The child who scores above 112 <u>may</u> in fact have certain qualities that set him apart from most of his peers, and this in turn might be a reasonable interpretation of the word "superior." But you can't justify this second use of the word superior just on the basis of a test score. The child might have been superior only at taking a certain kind of test on a certain day. And in any case, the trouble is that words can be misleading. What happens when we get a score <u>below</u> average? If we use the same statistical and verbal reasoning that leads us to label a score of 12 points over the mean as "superior," then we have no choice but to label a score of 12 points <u>below</u> the mean as "_____."

- -

inferior

38.   If we are talking about the score, not about the child himself, and <u>if</u> we define inferior to mean "statistically below average," then we could use the word "inferior" with the same justification as "superior."

"Inferior," however, is a loaded word. We simply don't use it in polite society. Instead, the word that is often used to characterize IQ scores between 88 and 76 is "dull."

But this may be even a poorer word than "inferior." How can you talk about a <u>score</u> as being "dull"? When this word is used--as it still is in many texts--it conjures up a picture of the child himself. It also carries connotations of qualities that may have little or nothing to do with intelligence.

The original justification for the use of the word "dull" was to distinguish this range of scores from those scores that might indicate that a child is "retarded." In general, "retarded" is a word used to describe children who will benefit more from special remedial education programs than from a regular school setting. One purpose of Alfred Binet's original test was to attempt to identify such children relatively early in life. A child who scores in the "dull" range, as opposed to "retarded," can usually function in a regular school setting.

Do you think that the words "retarded" and "dull" have other possible meanings and connotations (YES/NO)

- -

(Answer is discussed below.)

39.   Of course they do--and that is one of the big problems in the use (or misuse) of intelligence tests. We have seen that there is some reasonable justification for the use of the word "superior" on linguistic and statistical grounds, provided we keep in mind that it refers to the (SCORE/CHILD/BOTH).

- -

SCORE

40.   Yet this qualification usually is not kept in mind. Moreover, the other words we have been discussing ("retarded" and "dull") make it almost impossible to keep in mind the fact that an IQ score is only a statistical statement of how a child stands in regard to his reference population.

Another misleading word is "genius," which is often used in connection with an IQ score over 148. This word in its common English usage clearly refers to a (SCORE/PERSON).

- -

PERSON

41.   Moreover, when we think of the persons to whom the word has been applied, we usually think of persons who have actually achieved a magnificent body of work in some field, rather than persons who simply seem to have high potential.

It would be correct to say that a child who scores very high on an intelligence test has a higher probability of eventually becoming a genius than most children. But the probability itself is still quite low, and in any event there is no reason to consider 148 as a rigid "cut-off" point.

From information already given, you might want to guess why this particular number is often used. In terms of deviation IQ scores, what's so special about 148?

(Note: If you don't recall, look back at frame 12 in this chapter.)

_ _

It's three standard deviations above the mean.

42.   As you know, -3.0 and +3.0 are the points at which most normal curve tables end. It is simply not worth the time and trouble to differentiate between the 99.9 percentile and the 100th. Thus a "genius," according to this style of interpreting IQ scores, is someone whose score is so high that it cannot conveniently be found in a percentile table.

   If this sounds illogical, it's supposed to. We strongly recommend not using shorthand verbal descriptions from IQ tests or any tests. Even the statement "John is very tall" was open to qualification. We had to amend it to "John's height of 79 inches is in the 99th percentile of heights of all 16-year-old American boys."

   Let us now review and summarize our discussion of the IQ score. First we pointed out that it is the result of a test that has several components. These are usually in two categories: _____ and

_____.

_ _

verbal and nonverbal (or similar answer; the Wechsler terminology is "verbal" and "performance")

43.   Which of the following, if any, are true in regard to verbal and nonverbal IQ scores?

   (1) _____ A person who scores high in regard to one is likely to score high in regard to the other.
   (2) _____ Any difference between the two should be investigated.
   (3) _____ Verbal IQ is a better predictor than nonverbal IQ of success in school.
   (4) _____ Verbal IQ scores and nonverbal IQ scores cannot be averaged to yield a total IQ score.

_ _

(1) True. The technical way of stating it is that verbal and nonverbal scores are "positively correlated." We will discuss the "correlation" concept more fully in the next chapter.
(2) Not true. It is correct that a large discrepancy between verbal and nonverbal scores of the same person is worthy of investigation. If the difference is only a few points, however, it might be due to measurement error. As a rule of thumb, one standard deviation represents a difference that can be considered statistically significant.
(3) True. See discussion in frames 19-25 of this chapter.
(4) Not true. See frame 18 or any entry in Exhibit 7.

44.   Which of the following is true in regard to the term "IQ"?

(1) _____ Unless stated otherwise, you can assume that after 1960 an IQ score is a deviation IQ, not a ratio I.Q.

(2) _____ It stands for "intelligence qualities."

(3) _____ It stands for "intelligence quotient."

(4) _____ It is applicable only to the Stanford-Binet test; the use of the term in regard to other tests is not technically accurate.

(5) _____ If all persons in a given age group took the same intelligence test scored on a deviation IQ basis, the mean of all scores would be 100, or very close to it.

(6) _____ Ratio I.Q.'s and deviation IQ's are not comparable.

- -

(1) <u>True</u>. Ratio I.Q.'s are used only with the pre-1960 version of the Stanford-Binet test.

(2) (3) <u>Not true</u>. "IQ" without periods no longer stands for anything. It is used simply because we're used to it. This point was not stated in the text in these words, but it was emphasized that "quotient" is no longer applicable.

(4) <u>Not true</u>. Deviation IQ scores have the same meaning in terms of percentile equivalents in all tests in which they are used.

(5) <u>True</u>.

(6) <u>Not true</u>. As stated earlier (frame 4), the problems of the ratio I.Q. method are of a technical nature which do not drastically affect the meaning of an individual score. A person who scored, say, 117 on the old basis would probably have scored close to that if he had been scored on a deviation IQ basis.

These were tricky questions. If you correctly labeled the two true statements (1 and 5), don't feel bad if you were misled by one or even two of the others.

45.   Henry attains a total IQ score of 93 on an intelligence test. Assuming that the test itself is a good test of intelligence and that it is scored on a deviation IQ basis, how would you interpret this score?

_____ Below-average intelligence
_____ Average intelligence
_____ Stay away from the word "average" altogether

Give your reasons for accepting or rejecting each choice.

_____

_____

_____

- -

"Average intelligence" is probably the best answer, but reasons for and against each choice follow.

If you had to divide the entire population into "above average" or "below average," then you would have no choice but to interpret a score of 93 as "below average." In that case, however, nobody would be of "average" intelligence except for that very small fraction of the population that happens to score 100.0. Thus it is better to think of "average" as being a range of scores, such as 88 to 112 (or, as given in some texts, 90 to 110).

Another reason for deciding against "below average" is the possibility of measurement error. Even if you wanted to maintain 100 as a rigid cut-off point, there is a substantial possibility that on some other occasion Henry would score over 100.

Unlike most of the other words we have been discussing, "average" has a statistical meaning: 100 or close to it. The word to steer clear of is not "average," but "normal," which has many nonstatistical connotations. However, when you do use the word "average" or any word at all, be sure you are using it in connection with the score, not the child himself.

46.   The word "genius" is sometimes used in connection with a deviation IQ score above 148.

    (1) Why this particular number?

_____

    (2) What would be the corresponding score on the Wechsler scale?

_____

- -

(1) It is $+3.0$ standard deviations above the mean--the point at which most standard score tables end.
(2) 145 (Wechsler deviation IQ has a standard deviation of 15, not 16.)

47.   This question was only for the purpose of reviewing the standard deviation of IQ scores, not to justify the use of the term "genius." As discussed earlier, there is no justification for applying this word to a child on the basis of a test score.

We have been bearing down hard on some of the common misconceptions about the term "IQ"--but only in regard to intelligence tests in general. To go into the positive aspects of intelligence tests, or any kind of test, it is necessary to go beyond the scores themselves. In regard to any test, we have to ask the following questions:

    (1) Is the ability or trait itself (e.g., "intelligence" or "arithmetical aptitude") meaningful?
    (2) If so, does the test adequately measure it?
    (3) Does the test enable us to make predictions or judgments that are useful, accurate, and not obtainable in other ways?

These are some of the questions that relate to the topic of validity, which we will discuss in the next chapter.

TEST FOR CHAPTER 3

1. Donald's verbal IQ score is 121. What is the equivalent percentile rank? _____

2. We would expect that Donald's nonverbal score would be:

    _____ similarly high
    _____ average
    _____ below average
    _____ totally unrelated to his verbal IQ

3. Which of the following would probably be found in the verbal part of an intelligence test (as opposed to the nonverbal part)?

    _____ If John has 3 apples and Peggy has 4 oranges, how many pieces of fruit do they have together?
    _____ CLEVER means: _____ silly _____ smart _____ wicked
    _____ How many hours are there in a day?
    _____ All of the above
    _____ None of the above

4. Elaine's verbal IQ score is 107 and her nonverbal IQ score is 96. Is this difference considered statistically significant? (YES/NO) What is the reason for your answer? _____

    _____

5. How do the Lorge-Thorndike and other standardized group-administered intelligence tests differ from the Stanford-Binet?

    _____ They have different means and standard deviations.
    _____ They have fundamentally different conceptions of intelligence.
    _____ They do not require a trained examiner.
    _____ All of the above.
    _____ None of the above.

6. Fill in this table.

	MEAN IQ	SD
Wechsler scales	_____	_____
Stanford-Binet	_____	_____
All other tests scored on deviation IQ basis	_____	_____

7. Arthur took the Stanford-Binet test in 1958. His mental age was computed to be 84 months. His chronological age was 80 months. What was his Intelligence Quotient?

    _____ 95
    _____ 105
    _____ 84

8. Arthur's brother, Leonard, took the same test five years later. He scored one-half a standard deviation above the mean of all persons his age. What was his deviation IQ score?

   _____ 108
   _____ 115
   _____ 116
   _____ 132

9. If the boys' parents were informed of these scores, they might conclude that Leonard's IQ is higher than Arthur's. Why would they be wrong? (Note: If you are not certain of your answers to questions 7 and 8, look them up before tackling this question.)

   _____

   _____

   _____

   _____

10. "I've got a genius in my classroom," says Mr. Jones. "Katy Goodman scored 151 on the Stanford-Binet. I remember seeing somewhere that a score of more than 148 is in the 'genius' range." Mr. Jones probably did see it somewhere--but he's still wrong. Why? (Give at least two reasons.)

    _____

    _____

    _____

    _____

11. Dick's verbal IQ score is 114; nonverbal, 102. What is his total IQ score? _____ What percentile does this place him in? _____

12. The percentile rank you computed in question 11 refers to

    _____ all boys of Dick's age
    _____ all children of Dick's age
    _____ all boys of Dick's grade level
    _____ all children of Dick's grade level

Answers

1. Percentile rank: 90 $\quad (z = \dfrac{121 - 100}{16} = +1.3)$ (frames 6-10)
2. Similarly high (frames 23-25)
3. All of the above (frames 18-19)
4. NO. The rule of thumb is that a difference of one standard deviation (15 or 16 points) is considered significant, and the difference in this example is only 11. Consider yourself partly correct if you simply said that both scores seem to be close to the average score, which is correct though not exactly the point. (frames 23-24)

5.   They do not require a trained examiner. (frames 15-16)

6.

	MEAN IQ	SD
Wechsler	100	15
Stanford-Binet	100	16
Others	100	16

(frames 14-17, especially 17)

7.   105 ($\frac{84}{80}$ x 100 = 105). This choice could also have been arrived at by logic rather than computation. (frames 2-3)

8.   108 (the mean, 100, plus half a standard deviation, 8) (frames 7-9)

9.   The answer to avoid is that the old I.Q. (quotient) score and the newer deviation IQ score are not comparable with one another. The two types of scores generally are comparable (see frames 4 and 44), and in any case there are much better reasons for not assuming that Leonard's IQ is higher than Arthur's:

- Measurement error. On another occasion either boy could have scored a few points more or less.
- The difference between the two scores is not statistically significant.
- Both scores are in the average range.

Consider yourself correct if you simply said "the scores are essentially the same" or "the difference is not worth bothering about" or words to that effect. (See also frame 36.)

10.
- The genius range has been set at 148 quite arbitrarily; it's simply the score at which the normal curve table usually ends.
- Even if this point were of great significance, it is highly possible that on another occasion Katy might have scored below 148.
- If verbal labels are used at all, they should refer to the score, not the child (especially the word "genius," which implies a person who has already achieved a magnificent body of work in a particular field).

(frames 40-43)

11. Total IQ score: 108 (average of verbal and nonverbal scores)

Percentile rank: 69 ($z = \frac{108 - 100}{16} = +0.5$)

Note that computing percentiles for the verbal component and the nonverbal component, and then averaging the percentiles, is not only extra work but is incorrect. If you did this, see frame 2 and also the answer to question 7 in the test for Chapter 2.

12. All children of Dick's age (Deviation IQ percentiles are age percentiles, not grade percentiles. Both sexes are scored together.) (frames 15-16, 27-28)

CHAPTER FOUR

Validity

1.   Up to now we have been discussing mainly the <u>numerical</u> interpretation of test results. For example, suppose we are concerned
with a test of arithmetical ability. As we have seen from statistical
comparison of a score with the average score, we can conclude:

    _____ how much arithmetic a person knows
    _____ how he stands on that test in relation to others
           in a given reference population
    _____ how well he will be able to do in the future in
           schoolwork or other work requiring arithmetic

- - - - - - - - - - - - - - - - - - - -

On the basis of what we have discussed so far, the only answer is
"how he stands on that test in relation to others in a given reference
population."

2.   To make any other definitive conclusions, we must know more
than simply the distribution of scores. We have to know a good deal
about the test itself and the purposes for which it is to be used.
    The most obvious way to evaluate a test is for the teacher (or
other person making use of it) simply to look at it. Suppose, for example that we have a test designed to measure the student's familiar-
ity with, and understanding of, the great works of English literature.
There are essays and multiple-choice questions dealing with Tolstoi's
<u>War and Peace</u>, Flaubert's <u>Madame Bovary</u>, Goethe's <u>Faust</u>, and
Dostoevski's <u>Crime and Punishment</u>. No matter how penetrating the
questions themselves, we can rule out this test as a valid measure of
knowledge of English Literature just on the face of it. Why?

_____

- - - - - - - - - - - - - - - - - - - -

These are not works of <u>English</u> literature (or similar answer).

3.   This was an example of <u>face validity</u>--or rather, the absence of
it. If the purpose of the test is to measure the student's competence
in English literature, we could rule out this test just on the face of it.

Here is another example. The coach of the track team wants to select the best men to run cross-country. Which of the following kinds of test do you think would be valid, just on the face of it, for a "Cross-Country Aptitude Test"?

_____ answering a series of personality questions
_____ doing a number of arithmetic problems
_____ a general intelligence test
_____ a weight-lifting competition
_____ running the 100-yard dash

- -

(Answer is discussed below.)

4.   On the face of it, running the 100-yard dash is the only test that would be applicable. Yet even this is not a valid test of cross-country running. Endurance over several miles of rugged hilly country is actually quite a different thing than the speed required to do well in a 100-yard dash.

Actually, it <u>may</u> be that personality variables such as ego strength and low anxiety level are important characteristics of the long-distance runner. Also, general intelligence, weight lifting, and indeed (for all we know at this point) even arithmetical ability <u>may</u> have some positive relationship to cross-country running.

Thus, either accepting or rejecting a test simply "on the face of it" is not advisable as the sole procedure for determining the validity of a test. The person who uses a test should always look at it critically to get an idea of its face validity. Still, it is clear that a determination of <u>face validity</u> is generally based on:

_____ subjective impression
_____ research
_____ thorough analysis

- -

subjective impression

5.   There is nothing "wrong" with using subjective impressions, but certainly we need to do more. Let's go back to the example of the track coach for a moment. There is really nothing requiring him to use any test at all. He is the coach and he has the right to pick the athletes who in his opinion will perform the best. What are some possible reasons for his wanting to use any test at all?

_____

_____

_____

You might have said that a test, rather than an arbitrary choice, would be more <u>fair</u> to the athletes involved, or that it would give the coach more <u>information</u> on which to base his choice, or other reasons. In any case, the purpose of a test is clearly to <u>reduce</u> the reliance on subjective impression and guesswork. Thus it hardly makes sense to use impressionistic thinking in assessing the validity of a test.

6.   Simply to review the technical term that you will encounter in many books on testing, the kind of validity that is inferred from just looking at the test, to see if it generally makes sense, is known as "_____" validity.

"face" validity

7.   What is important, of course, is not what the test looks like but whether the test results will tell us anything about what people will be likely to do on other tests or in nontesting situations.
    For example, as we have already seen, the Scholastic Aptitude Test is used by colleges in deciding on admissions. If the test is to be any use to them, it should be a valid test of scholastic aptitude. The mere fact that it is <u>called</u> a test of scholastic aptitude does not mean that it actually <u>is</u> one.
    If this test is a valid test for college work, what would we predict about people who do well on it, compared to people who do poorly?

_____

They will do better in college (or similar answer).

8.   And in fact, they generally do. The same relationship between test performance and achievement in college holds for a similar test of scholastic aptitude, the ACT (American College Testing) battery.
    This is an example of <u>criterion-related validity</u>, the most important of all concepts relating to validity of a test. A criterion (plural: criteria) is a standard by which we judge performance. What is the criterion in the example just used?

        _____ the student's score on the Scholastic Aptitude test
        _____ the student's grades in college

----

the student's grades in college

9.   You might wish to argue that there are, or should be, other criteria besides grades for judging success in college. Perhaps you would be right. Our problem, however, is not how to structure college admissions policies, but simply how to validate the Scholastic Aptitude Test. The <u>best</u> way to do so is to:

_____   see if it actually predicts what it is supposed to predict
_____   look at the test and see if it seems to be a good test of scholastic aptitude

- -

see if it actually predicts what it is supposed to predict

10.   Let's go back to our track coach. Assume he does decide to use some kind of test to decide which of his runners will compete in the cross-country runs. No matter what kind of <u>test</u> he uses, what is the <u>criterion</u> according to which he will be able to tell whether his selection procedure was sound?

_____

- -

How well the runners do in the actual cross-country competition (or similar answer)

11.   Let's say that the coach's test consists of having each athlete lift weights, hold his breath as long as he can, and run a 100-yard dash. The test score could be some combination of how well he does in all three events.
       Later, in the first cross-country race of the season, the coach enters six runners--three who did very well on the test and three who did relatively poorly. Suppose it turns out that the latter three all do <u>better</u> than the ones who scored high on the test.
       The coach would have to infer that, in regard to cross-country running, his test (DOES/DOES NOT) have "<u>criterion-related validity</u>"; or in other words, in regard to predicting the performance that he is interested in, the coach's test is (VALID/INVALID).

- -

DOES NOT
INVALID

12.   Let's illustrate these same points with an example from industrial testing. Suppose you have a test that is designed to help hire success-ful salesmen while screening out those who would not be successful. The test is designed to assess the degree to which the person enjoys being with and talking with people, his ability to make quick decisions involving numerical data, and his ability to be patient even when some-one is arguing with him. Assume that these qualities are important to a salesman, and that on inspecting the test you feel that it does actually measure them. After a few years, however, it becomes apparent that salesmen who have done very well on this test do not have better sales records than salesmen who have done poorly on the test.

Given all these facts we would conclude that this test has:

_____   face validity
_____   criterion-related validity
_____   both
_____   neither

- -

face validity but not criterion-related validity

13.   We would say it has face validity because, on the face of it, the test seemed to be a good one, but since it did not adequately predict who would do well as a salesman, it did not have criterion-related validity.

To make sure you understand the concept of criterion-related validity, what was the criterion in this example?

_____   how well the persons did on the test
_____   their actual ability to make quick decisions, be
          patient, and enjoy talking to people
_____   their sales performance after they were hired

- -

their sales performance after they were hired

14.   Now you're the manager deciding whether to continue using this test. What would you do in the face of the evidence?

_____   continue using the test, since it appears to measure
          those factors that have to do with sales success
_____   discontinue using the test, since it is not serving its
          purpose of predicting performance

- -

discontinue (Of course the same logic would apply to a teacher, psychologist, school administrator, or anyone deciding whether to use a particular test.)

15.   From all these examples, we can generalize that criterion-related validity is the most important kind of validity. In other words, (1) if a test can actually predict what it is designed to predict, it should be considered "valid" even if it doesn't look valid on the face of it; and (2) if it does not predict what it is designed to predict, there is no point in using it no matter what other grounds you may have for believing that it is a "good test."

Our examples so far have been illustrating the second point made above; now here's one to illustrate the first. In the last 10 or 20 years, the identification of potentially creative people has become an important concern of many psychologists and educators. In one well-known test of creative potential, the subject (the person who takes the test) is given three common words such as "bureau," "treasure," and "torso." His task is to find a fourth word that is somehow associated with them. The answer is "chest."

The test consists of many items of this kind (the one given does not appear on the actual test), which have to be answered in a fairly short time limit.

Now let's ask ourselves about the validity of such a test, considered as a test of "creativity." Although we cannot begin to raise all the issues pertaining to creativity, or to give answers to even some of them, it is certainly safe to say that creativity:

(1) involves being unique or original rather than simply coming up with the "right" answer
(2) is often nonverbal
(3) is not usually associated with working under time pressure

Given the discussion so far, and the points listed above, does this test seem, on the face of it, to be a valid measure of creativity? (YES/NO/MAYBE)

- -

There is no originality called for, since there is only one right answer and everybody who gets the right answer gives the same one. It is obviously a verbally oriented test, and there is a certain amount of time pressure. So the answer is NO, or possibly MAYBE, but certainly not YES--at least not on the face of it.

16.   As we have seen, however, face validity is of virtually no importance. Let's consider the criterion-related validity of the test. For example, the production of new scientific inventions would have to be considered one good criterion of creativity. Suppose, then, that a sample of 29 scientists was divided into two groups: those who scored high on this test and those who scored low (relative to the first group). Of all the patents that had been granted to these 29 scientists, 93 percent of them had been granted to those in the high-scoring group. Putting aside purely statistical questions such as the small size of the sample, would you consider this to be indicative of criterion-related validity? (YES/NO)

YES (assuming that the production of scientific inventions is at least one suitable criterion for "creativity")

17.   This was an example of a validity study. Although you may not undertake validity studies yourself, you will undoubtedly read many such studies if you have anything to do with the selection or evaluation of published tests. Understanding what is involved in such a study is probably the best way to understand the concept of criterion-related validity.
The first step in a validity study is:

(1) Specify what the test is supposed to measure--for example, arithmetical ability, intelligence, knowledge of English literature, mechanical aptitude, or (as in the preceding example) creativity.

Of course, as we have seen, the fact that a test is called a test of something-or-other:

_____ is a good indication that it actually does measure what it claims to measure
_____ is no indication that it actually measures what it claims to measure
_____ is a partial indication that it actually measures what it claims to measure

----

no indication

18.   You cannot have even a partial indication that the test is actually measuring what it says it is measuring without the second step in a validity study:

(2) Establish a criterion that indicates the presence or absence of what is being tested.

The criterion in the study just mentioned was "scientific patents granted." Which of the following do you think might be considered suitable criteria that might tend to differentiate persons of relatively high and relatively low creativity?

_____ Performance in extracurricular activities such as a school orchestra, newspaper, or chess team
_____ Grades achieved in school subjects
_____ Success in certain occupations such as art, architecture, music, writing
_____ Performance on the creativity test that you are trying to validate

----

Performance in extracurricular activities such as
a school orchestra, newspaper, or chess team
Success in certain occupations such as art, architecture, music, writing

19.   In regard to the other answers, there is no evidence that grades
in school have anything to do with creativity; in fact, there is some
evidence to indicate that within a group of people of equal intelligence,
the more creative person will tend to get somewhat poorer grades.
(Of course you are not expected to know this just from what you have
read in this book.)
       Performance on that very test cannot be considered a criterion
because then you would simply be comparing the test with itself, not
with some outside standard.
       The other two criteria have been used in validity studies of cre-
ativity tests. This doesn't mean that they are the best criteria to use,
and of course there are many other possibilities.
       Our purpose here is only to discuss the concept of the relationship
between a test and a criterion, not to get into the question of creativity
itself. Some references to this subject are given in the bibliography.

(No answer necessary.)

20.   In review, the first three steps in a validity study are:

   (1) Specify the dimension of interest--that is, arithmetical
       ability, creativity, intelligence, cross-country ability,
       musical knowledge, scholastic aptitude, or anything that
       the test is supposed to measure.
   (2) Establish a criterion that will define the degree to which
       people are "high" or "low" in this dimension of interest.
   (3) Make a prediction as to how the test results will be related
       to criterion performance.

The next steps, which we will now discuss, are:

   (4) Administer the test to a selected sample of persons, some
       of whom are high on the criterion and some of whom are low.
   (5) Analyze the results. If the test is to be considered valid,
       then those who are high on the criterion should generally
       tend to score (HIGH/LOW) on the test.

HIGH

21.   The technical way of stating the same thing is to say that if the test has criterion-related validity, then the test scores should <u>correlate</u> with criterion performance. The actual degree to which this relationship is true can be stated in terms of a <u>correlation coefficient</u>.
     In the remainder of this chapter we will review some aspects of criterion-related validity and also show how it is measured in terms of a correlation coefficient.

(<u>No answer necessary.</u>)

(Note: Here is the best place to take a break in this chapter.)

22.   Suppose we want to validate a new intelligence test, which we'll call the "Hypothetical Test of Intellectual Ability" (HTIA). The test is designed to measure the capacity of high-school students to do academic work, so that guidance counselors will be better equipped to advise students on their course of study--vocational, technical, college preparatory, etc.
     Since we are only illustrating the concept of validity as a statistical correlation between test scores and a criterion, we are not concerned with whether there "should" or "should not" be different kinds of programs in high school. Nor is it implied that one test alone provides sufficient information to make such an important decision.
     Our problem, although narrower, is still quite broad, for we are trying to answer the fundamental question pertaining to the validity of a test: Does it really measure what it is supposed to measure ? One way to answer this is to compare the results on the test with performance on something measurable outside the testing situation. This "something measurable" is known as the _____.

- -

criterion

23.   We would like to validate this test against a readily measurable criterion which satisfies us that the test is really measuring "intellectual ability" and, more importantly, convinces us that the test is suitable for the particular purpose it is designed for. What we will do, then, is to compare the results on the Hypothetical Test of Intellectual Ability with academic grade averages. (We will not include gym, art, or other nonacademic courses.)
     If we assume that this test is somewhat similar in purpose and content to the SAT College Board (but on the high-school level), we would predict that students who do well on it will tend to get (HIGHER/LOWER) academic grades than students who do less well.

- -

HIGHER

24.   To test this prediction, ideally we would use a large sample of
students (in the thousands) from across the country. To keep this
example simple, however, we will assume that we are doing a study
in only one school, using only 30 students.

Hypothetical results for this sample of students are shown in Exhibit 9 on page 134. Just looking at the intelligence-test scores (column 2), it would appear that they are in terms of:

_____ deviation IQ's
_____ raw test scores
_____ age equivalents

_ _

raw test scores

25.   We need not go into the reasons for using raw scores. The previous question was simply a review designed to test your ability to make
guesses as to what numbers mean. In our study of the IQ scores in
Exhibit 7 we found several occasions where this kind of numerical
guesswork is necessary!

Now let us consider the results themselves. Based on this sample,
what would you guess as to the relationship between the test scores and
school grades?

_____ They seem to be correlated.
_____ They do not seem to be correlated .
_____ There is no way to determine the answer just
         from looking at the data.

_ _

(Answer is discussed below.)

26.   From the data in Exhibit 9 it would appear that, in general, students who score high on the test are getting higher grades in school than
students who score lower on the test. For example, most of the students whose test scores are high (in the 40's) have grade averages in
the 80's or 90's, while most students whose test scores are low have
grade averages in the 60's or 70's. Thus it is correct to say that the
test scores and grades "seem to be correlated."

In order to make sure of this point, however, we need to be more
precise. Inspection of the data can sometimes be deceptive. Thus you
are also correct if you said that "there is no way to determine the answer just from looking at the data," or if you gave both these answers.

One way to get a clearer picture of the data is to portray the results graphically, as shown in Exhibit 10 (page 135). Notice that the
horizontal axis represents test scores; the vertical axis represents
criterion performance (grade averages).

Since the bottom limit for both raw test scores and grade averages is 0, the two axes should intersect at a zero point. However, to save space without changing the results, the origin of our graph (the point where the axes intersect) begins at the lowest scores actually achieved, rather than the lowest possible scores.

Simply to make sure you understand how the points were plotted, consider the dot in the extreme upper-right corner of the graph. This dot represents a raw score on the intelligence test of _____ , and a grade average of _____ . The dot represents the performance of student number _____ in Exhibit 9.

- -

48, 96
Student #8

27.   In general, the points in the upper-right section of the graph represent students who are doing well on both the test and the criterion (grade average). Points in the lower-left area represent students who:

_____   score high on the test but have low grade averages
_____   score high on the test and have high grade averages
_____   score low on the test and have low grade averages
_____   score low on the test and have high grade averages

- -

score low on the test and have low grade averages
(If you are quite familiar with the concept of the "correlation coefficient" and its numerical representation, you may skip or skim rapidly to frame 37, second paragraph.)

28.   Using a little bit of visual imagination, we can consider all the points on the graph to be located near an imaginary line that runs from the lower left to the upper right (or from the upper right to the lower left). This is evidence of a positive correlation between test scores and grade averages because, in general, what the graph shows is that:

_____   the higher one's test score, the higher one's grade average
_____   the higher one's test score, the lower one's grade average
_____   the lower one's test score, the higher one's grade average
_____   the lower one's test score, the lower one's grade average

- -

the higher one's test score, the higher one's grade average
and/or
the lower one's test score, the lower one's grade average

29.   Suppose the results had turned out to be different, such that high test scores were associated with low grade averages, and vice versa. Which of the following graphs would show this relationship? (1/2/3)

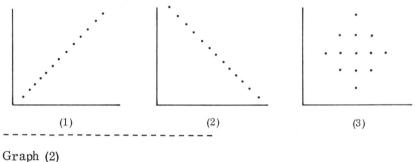

(1)   (2)   (3)

- -

Graph (2)

30.   There is still a third possibility--namely, that there is no relationship of any kind between scores on this intelligence test and grade averages.

This possibility is shown by graph (3) in the preceding frame. Explain why graph (3) shows <u>no</u> correlation, rather than either a positive or a negative correlation:

_____

_____

- -

(Answer is given below.)

31.   In visual terms, what this means is that persons who are scoring high on the test may have <u>high</u> grade averages, <u>moderate</u> averages, or <u>low</u> averages. Similarly, persons who have high averages may score high, low, or moderate on the test.

Either of the two above answers is good. The best answer, which has been hinted at but not expressly stated, is that graph (3) shows that <u>there is no way of making a prediction of a person's grade average</u> based on scores on the test.

Considering the above, which of the following results would cast doubt on the validity of our Hypothetical Test of Intellectual Ability?

_____ positive correlation with grade averages
_____ negative correlation with grade averages
_____ no correlation with grade averages

- -

negative correlation or no correlation (Both should be checked, but either one can be considered correct.)

32.   In general, then, there are three types of correlation: positive correlation, no correlation, and negative correlation. In this particular case, where we predicted that the high scores on the test would be associated with high grade averages, the positive correlation that we obtained (Exhibit 10) is evidence (FOR/AGAINST) the validity of the Hypothetical Test of Intellectual Ability.

- -

FOR

33.   Up to now we have mentioned three possibilities--<u>positive</u>, <u>negative</u>, and <u>no</u> correlation. The first two graphs in frame 29 represent a perfect positive and a perfect negative correlation, because the results form a perfectly straight line. The third graph represents a zero correlation, because the points are distributed symmetrically all over the graph.
       In real life, we almost never obtain such symmetry. We invariably find that we have either a positive correlation <u>to some degree</u>, or a negative correlation <u>to some degree</u>. The graph in Exhibit 10 would seem to indicate:

_____ a perfect positive correlation
_____ a positive correlation to some degree
_____ no correlation
_____ a negative correlation to some degree
_____ a perfect negative correlation

- -

a positive correlation to some degree (as discussed in frame 28)

34.   A positive correlation is expressed numerically as a two-decimal number ranging between 0.00 and +1.00. For example, the correlation between the Hypothetical Test of Intellectual Ability score and academic grade averages achieved in high school, as shown in Exhibit 10, is +.57 (as derived by a mathematical formula which we are not going into).
       Within the scope of this book we cannot cover the details of what this number actually means. What we will do is give a few examples that might help you develop a "feel" for the significance of correlation coefficients.
       Suppose that our sample had contained 33 students instead of 30, and that the three additional students had achieved the following results:

Student	HTIA Score	Grade Average
31	25	92
32	36	64
33	46	80

First, as an optional exercise, plot these points on your graph in Exhibit 10 and put a circle around them. Then look at Exhibit 11, which shows the same graph with these new points added.

(No answer necessary.)

35.   The three circled points in Exhibit 11 represent the results of the three additional students. Looking again at these points, or at the figures themselves in the preceding frame, we note that the first student has a very low test score and a high grade average, the second has a fair test score and a low average, while the third has a high test score and only a fair grade average.

With the original 30 students (Exhibit 10), the correlation coefficient was +.57. This is a fairly high positive correlation. Now, considering all 33 students (Exhibit 11), what effect would these additional results have on the correlation coefficient?

_____ It would be increased to some number between +.57 and 1.00.
_____ It would be decreased to some number below +.57.

- -

It would be decreased to some number below +.57.

36.   Let's go one step farther. Given that Exhibit 11 shows less of a correlation than Exhibit 10, how much less?

_____ less than +.57, but still above 0; in other words, a positive correlation but less positive than before
_____ below 0; that is, a negative correlation

- -

less than +.57, but still above 0; in other words, a positive correlation but less positive than before

37.   The reason for this answer is that although these three results do not fit the general pattern, all 33 students taken as a whole still show a general trend from the lower left to the upper right. As it happens, the mathematical formula for the correlation coefficient from the Exhibit 11 data results in a correlation coefficient of +.25, which is substantially lower than +.57 but substantially higher than zero.

The correlation coefficient is always symbolized by the letter "r." Suppose that in a study that compares results on a spelling test to results on a reading test, $r = +.27$. This means that, insofar as these abilities are actually measured by these tests,

_____ the better one reads, the worse one spells, and vice versa
_____ there is no connection between spelling ability and reading ability

(continued)

_____ there is a relatively mild relationship between
spelling ability and reading ability
_____ there is a strong relationship between spelling
ability and reading ability

- -

The important point was to eliminate the first answer--"the better one
reads, the worse one spells, and vice versa." This could be stated
only if the correlation were negative; however, in this example r was
given as positive (+.27).

It would also be incorrect, but not <u>as</u> incorrect, to say that with r
equal to +.27, "there is no connection between spelling ability and reading ability." Actually we might expect, on commonsense grounds, a
higher correlation and we cannot really tell what the number means
unless we know the size of the sample and many other facts, but we
can say that there is quite a difference between 0.00 and +.27--enough
to indicate that there is some relationship.

Technically, the best answer is that "there is a relatively mild relationship between spelling ability and reading ability." However, we
cannot go into why this is the best answer, and under some circumstances +.27 could be interpreted as a strong relationship. Consider
yourself correct if you gave either of these two answers.

If you were incorrect and skipped originally, go back to frame 28,
page 77.

38.   A rule of thumb that is often given is that in validity studies, when
positive correlations have been predicted between the test and a criterion, the actual correlations should turn out to be between +.20 and
+.60 (Lyman, 1971, p. 46; see also Cronbach, 1970, p. 135). However, there is nothing sacred about either of these numbers. The best
way to get a feel for what correlation coefficients mean is to look at
some typical examples. A few are seen in Exhibit 12 (page 137).
Please note that these results are only those that were obtained in particular research projects; other studies might show different results.

After looking at Exhibit 12, label the following statements <u>true</u> or
<u>false</u> (assuming that we can generalize from this one Exhibit, which we
can):

_____ If no sign (+ or -) is given in front of the correlation
coefficient, it is assumed to be plus.
_____ In this context, the word "versus" can be taken as
synonymous with "compared with."
_____ Correlation coefficients can be computed for any two
sets of data, including those that have nothing to do
with "tests" in the usual sense.

- -

All are true.

39.   Now let's inspect some of the correlations. Consider "Height versus Binet IQ." This, of course, is shorthand. What it means is:

In a certain validity study, the heights of a sample of persons were recorded. Their IQ scores on the Stanford–Binet test were also recorded. When the formula for the correlation coefficient was applied to the data, r was found to be equal to +.06.

(1) How would you interpret this result?

_____ A person's height is a good indicator of his intelligence.
_____ There is little or no relationship between height and intelligence.

(2) If we graphed the data from this study, which one would it look like? (A/B/C)

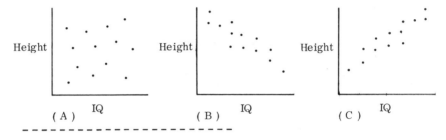

Height (A)   IQ   Height (B)   IQ   Height (C)   IQ

- -

(1) There is little or no relationship between height and intelligence.
(2) Graph A

40.   This result is what we would expect from common sense and from all other research. Thus if we found a strong relationship, either positive or negative, between results on an intelligence test and height, we might become doubtful about the validity of the test. Consider the following fictitious example:

A test of intelligence for preschool children consisted of identifying common objects, naming their colors, classifying them into certain categories, and physically rearranging them according to certain instructions. The correlation between these results on this test and height of the children turned out to be positive (r = .48). The correlation between this test and reading ability (measured two years later) was also positive (r = .31).

Would you say that this test has <u>face</u> validity? (YES/NO) Explain your answer:

_____

_____

--- --- --- --- --- --- --- --- --- --- --- --- -

YES
On the face of it, these tasks appear to be indicative of intelligence in preschool children. (Other answers discussed below.)

41.   In this example, your answer depends on your explanation. If you feel that these tasks are not good indicators of intelligence, then (whether you are right or wrong in this opinion) to you, the test does not have face validity and you could have answered NO. However, if you answered either YES or NO based on the correlation coefficients, you forgot the meaning of "face" validity, which has nothing to do with results--only with a general impression based on inspection of the test (or, as in this case, an inspection of the description of a test).

Read the example once again and assume that, in general, children who are more intelligent at preschool ages are more likely to be better readers than children who are less intelligent. Would you say that there is evidence of criterion-related validity? (YES/NO)

--- --- --- --- --- --- --- --- --- --- --- --- -

YES (A correlation of .31 is certainly "some evidence," though perhaps not as strong as we would like, that test performance and criterion performance are related. If you answered NO, review frame 38.)

42.   But now we have a problem. A psychologist assigned to evaluate this test became suspicious. Why, she asked herself, should there be such a high correlation between test results and height? An unexpected correlation like this casts doubt on the entire validity study, or possibly on the test itself. Investigating the details of the study, which had been reported in a journal article, she discovered that when the test materials were laid out, they were placed not on the floor but on a shelf.

As a result, some children who were intelligent but short had a problem. Without this problem these children would have done better on the intelligence test. These same children did do well on the reading test two years later. They should have scored higher on the intelligence test, and would have had it been properly administered. In that case, the correlation between the intelligence test and reading ability would have been:

_____ greater than .31
_____ smaller than .31
_____ unaffected

--- --- --- --- --- --- --- --- --- --- --- --- -

greater than .31

43.   This example illustrates a point that you are certain to run across in advanced work on tests and measurements: Mistakes of any kind will usually tend to reduce validity coefficients. That is certainly true in this (fictitious) example, in which there was a <u>systematic</u> error with a built-in bias against certain intelligent children. But this principle holds even for <u>random</u> errors. Suppose, for example, that the testing room is extremely noisy. We might think at first that this problem is the same for everyone and therefore should not affect the correlation coefficient. But it does! If the test really is a valid one, we want all conditions to be perfect. Nothing should affect the results except the students' actual ability. The greater the extent to which extraneous factors enter the situation, the less likely it is that we will observe a genuine relationship if one really exists.

<u>(No answer necessary.)</u>

44.   A correlation coefficient that results from comparing a test with a criterion is known as a validity coefficient. Some typical validity coefficients in Exhibit 13 indicate the important fact that in order to validate a test, it should be correlated with several different criteria, not just one. For example, consider the relationship between "word knowledge" and "success as a stenographer." What kind of correlation would you expect between these two variables?

_____ positive
_____ negative
_____ none

Explain your answer:

_____

_____

- -

positive
The better a stenographer's word knowledge, the better he or she will be able to take dictation, transcribe notes, make fewer spelling mistakes, etc.

45.   What kind of correlation would you expect between "word knowledge and "ability to operate a bookkeeping machine"?

_____ positive
_____ negative
_____ none

Explain your answer:

_____

_____

- -

(Answer is discussed below.)

46. "None" is probably the best answer, because operation of a book-keeping machine is primarily a <u>digital</u> skill. Moreover, the machine operator works almost entirely with numbers, not words. On the other hand, there is <u>some</u> reading ability involved in looking at the invoices and then punching the appropriate data in the machine. Thus we might expect a positive correlation, but a very slight one.

And that is exactly the result we get, as shown in Exhibit 13 ($r = .10$). Thus either "positive" or "none" was a good answer, if you had the right explanation.

We also see from Exhibit 13 that, as expected, the correlation between "word knowledge" and "success as a stenographer" (as measured by the job grade they attained--junior, senior, etc.) was highly positive ($r = .53$).

Both of these correlations bring joy to the heart of the test publisher, for they indicate not only that the test is doing what it is supposed to do, but also that it isn't doing what it isn't supposed to do. If high results on the "word knowledge" test predicted success on any kind of job, it would still be valuable, but not as <u>valid</u>. For then we might suspect that it really isn't word knowledge itself that is important, but some other factor that was responsible for the success of both machine operators and stenographers.

This was an example of the same test--word knowledge--in relation to two different criteria: success as stenographer and success as machine operator. Now let's consider the same criterion--success as stenographer--in relation to two different tests.

Which do you think should have a higher correlation with success as a stenographer?

_____ word knowledge
_____ arithmetic ability
_____ they should have equally high correlations

Explain your answer:

_____

_____

- -

word knowledge
Stenographers work much more with words than with numbers (or similar answer).

47.   In Exhibit 13, however, we find that this is not the case.   The correlation between "arithmetic skill" and "stenographic success" is higher (.60 as opposed to .53).

This is not the kind of finding that brings joy to a test publisher's heart.   The Short Employment Test would look more valid if we had a lower correlation, perhaps even a zero correlation, between arithmetic ability and success as a stenographer--given the assumption that arithmetic ability really has little to do with on-the-job success as a stenographer.

The conclusion that might well be drawn from these data is that success as a stenographer results not from separate verbal and arithmetical abilities, or from either one, but simply from general intelligence.   In that case we might be better off giving our stenographic applicants a general intelligence test.

We started, then, with a question of criterion-related validity: Does a test predict success or failure on some outside criterion?   Our tool for answering this question is the correlation coefficient between the test and the criterion.   However, we cannot stop there.   If we obtain the expected correlation, we have to determine if the relationship between the test and the criterion really has to do with what the test claims to be measuring, rather than simply with general intelligence, test-taking ability, working well under pressure, or other factors.   As opposed to such things as "arithmetic ability," "word knowledge," etc., those mentioned in the last sentence are (GENERAL/SPECIFIC) abilities.

- -

GENERAL

48.   One of the most important questions we have to ask about any test is whether it is measuring the specific ability it claims to be measuring, some other specific ability, a general ability, or a combination.

This is the question of construct validity.   (In this context, "construct" is a noun, pronounced "KON-struct.")   The idea behind this concept is that abilities, aptitudes, traits, characteristics, etc. do not really "exist" in the human organism, but are constructs (that is, ideas) that we have developed to explain the fact that people consistently do better on some kinds of tests than on others.

We cannot get into the philosophical and mathematical issues involved in the question of construct validity, although we will touch on it again in the next chapter.   The important thing to remember (as an aid in your future reading) is that "construct validity" refers to which of the following questions:

_____ Does the test enable us to make predictions?
_____ Is the test really measuring some specific characteristic?
_____ Does the test seem to be a good one?
_____ Is the test actually a good one?

- -

Is the test really measuring some specific characteristic?

49.   One other aspect of validity is known as <u>content validity</u>. This simply refers to whether the actual content of the test--the questions, tasks, etc.--are well chosen to achieve their objective of actually measuring the ability in question.

We will discuss content validity briefly in the next chapter, but generally will pass over it because in comparison to the other aspects of tests and measurements that we are discussing, it is relatively accessible to common sense and is something you can read about on your own.

In general, then, there is no such thing as a test being "valid" or "invalid." There are different <u>types</u> of validity, applicable to different <u>purposes</u> of a test, with varying degrees of evidence.

In the next chapter we will see that the same type of thinking has to be brought to bear on another important topic in tests and measurements: "reliability."

(<u>No answer necessary.</u>)

TEST FOR CHAPTER 4

1.   In a (fictitious) research experiment, a group of students study French and Spanish intensively for several years. Assume that the caliber of instruction, time spent, and other such factors are equal for both languages. At the end of the three-year period the students take proficiency tests in both languages. The correlation coefficient between the two sets of test results turns out to be .03.

(a) The result described above is shown by which of the following three graphs ? (A/B/C)

French scores | ... | Spanish scores — Graph 1
French scores | ... | Spanish scores — Graph 2
French scores | ... | Spanish scores — Graph 3

(b) The correlation coefficient of .03, and the graph that you gave as the answer to question (a), would be examples of:

_____ positive correlation
_____ negative correlation
_____ no correlation

(c) Which statement is indicated by the correlation of .03 ?

_____ The better a person learns Spanish, the more likely he is to learn French well.
_____ The better a person does in French, the worse he will do in Spanish.
_____ There is no relationship between ability to learn French and ability to learn Spanish.

(d) Suppose that the study was undertaken in order to investigate the question of whether there is a generalized ability to learn foreign languages. (Assume for purposes of this example that the correlation coefficient of .03 is a result that would be the case for all languages.) Which statement would be supported by this result?

_____ There is no such thing as "language aptitude." If there is any "aptitude," it is for the specific language rather than languages in general.

_____ Some people are good at learning foreign languages-- it doesn't matter which language.

2. A psychologist came to a kindergarten classroom to administer a test called the "Anderson Test of Athletic Ability." The test consists of drawing a picture of a common object, singing back a melody played on the piano, and counting backward from 10 to one. Through a complex method which we need not describe, each child ends up with a single result between 0 and 100.

(a) What can we reasonably say at this time?

_____ the test does not have face validity
_____ the test does not have criterion-related validity
_____ neither
_____ both

(b) Prior to giving the test, the psychologist had asked the school's physical-education teacher to rate each child in class on his or her athletic ability on a scale of 0 to 100. (For purposes of this question, ignore the question of sex differences.) Assume that the physical-education teacher knows all the children well and that his ratings are an accurate and acceptable criterion of athletic ability. The correlation coefficient between the test and the athletic ability ratings turns out to be .58. (This is to be considered a high positive correlation.) Now what would we say?

_____ the test has face validity
_____ the test has criterion-related validity
_____ neither
_____ both

(c) In a journal article describing this study, you read the following:

"We are willing to accept the physical-education teacher's ratings as good indicators of actual athletic ability. We can find no flaw with the statistical procedures and concede that the correlation coefficient is not a result of chance. However, it is well known that, at this age, children who are well developed in some abilities are likely to be well developed in others as well. We would expect to find similarly high correlations between this test and tests of intelligence, reading readiness, emotional adjustment, popularity with peers, and many other variables.

No matter what the predictive power of this test, we are
dubious that it is genuinely a valid test of 'athletic ability.
If the test shows us anything, it is that there may be no
such thing as 'athletic ability' as distinct from 'general
development.' "

Whether or not you agree with the authors, they seem to be
attacking the test on the ground (ground<u>s</u>, if you think more
than one) of:

_____ face validity
_____ construct validity
_____ criterion-related validity

(d) The teacher of this group of students makes his own ratings
of the athletic ability of the children, without knowing either
the test results or the ratings given by the physical-education
teacher. The correlation between her ratings and the physical-education teacher's ratings turns out to be .41. What is
the meaning of this result?

_____ The two teachers generally agree in their evaluations
of athletic ability, although not completely.
_____ There is virtually no relationship between the ratings
given by the classroom teacher and the ratings given
by the physical-education teacher.
_____ Those children who are rated "high" in athletic ability
by one of the teachers tend to be rated "low" by the
other.

(e) One day the classroom teacher wants to divide the class into
two groups--one high in athletic ability, and one low in athletic ability. She wants to consult the physical-education
teacher, but he is not available. However, the "Anderson
Test" results are available and it is no trouble to pick out
the 20 highest scorers and the 20 lowest. Would this procedure be advisable as a means of dividing the class according
to athletic ability? (As stated in part (d) above, the correlation between the test and the physical-education teacher's ratings, .41.)

_____ No--that test obviously has nothing to do with athletic
ability.
_____ No, because she can probably do better using her own
judgment as to athletic ability.
_____ Yes, because the results and discussion so far indicate that the test is a valid test of athletic ability.
_____ Yes, because the correlation of .58 indicates that the
higher a person's score on the test, the more likely
he is to be rated high in athletic ability by the physical-education teacher.

3. Which of the following is true about a "negative correlation" between a test score and a criterion? (Label each True or False.)

_____ It is indicated by graph 1 in question 1 above.

_____ It describes a situation in which persons who score high on the test would generally tend to score low on the criterion, or vice versa.

_____ It describes a situation in which there is <u>no</u> relationship between scores on the test and scores on the criterion.

4. If you see a correlation coefficient of .65, how would you know it is positive?

_____ because although it is lower than 1.00, it is higher than zero

_____ because if no sign appears before the correlation coefficient, a plus sign is understood

_____ both of the above

_____ neither--it is a negative correlation (less than 1.00)

_____ none of the above--it is close enough to zero to be considered <u>no</u> correlation

Answers

1. (a) Graph C (frames 30-31)
   (b) No correlation (frame 31)
   (c) There is no relationship between ability to learn French and and ability to learn Spanish. (frames 40-41)
   (d) There is no such thing as "language aptitude." If there is any "aptitude," it is for the specific language rather than languages in general.
   <u>Explanation</u>: If there were such a thing as "language aptitude" (or if the other statement in the question were correct), then we would expect a high correlation between the French test results and the Spanish test results. (This was not covered directly, but see frames 28-36, especially if you skipped them originally.)

2. (a) the test does not have face validity (It does not seem on the face of it to be a good test of athletic ability.)
   (It is incorrect to draw any conclusions about criterion-related validity, since no criterion has been specified and no statistical comparison has been made between test scores and performance on a criterion.) (frames 1-15, especially 2-4 and 12-14)
   (b) the test has criterion-related validity (The correlation coefficient between the test and criterion was high, and there was no question about the criterion itself.) (frames 7-15)
   (c) construct validity (The authors accepted the criterion and the statistical result as valid, and admitted that the test has "predictive power." They said nothing about the face validity of the test.) (frames 47-49)
   (d) The two teachers generally agree in their evaluations of athletic ability, although not completely. (In other words, those ranked high by one will <u>generally</u> be ranked high by the other. See frames 25-28 for the meaning of "positive correlation.")

(e) Yes, because the correlation of .58 indicates that the higher a person scores on the test, the more likely he is to be rated high in athletic ability by the physical-education teacher. Explanation (not required as part of your answer): In the absence of the physical-education teacher, the problem is to come up with a division into two groups that would most closely approximate what he would do. The teacher's own ratings were in some agreement with his (r = .42), but the "Anderson Test" results were even more highly correlated with his ratings of athletic ability (r = .58). Thus the above answer is correct and, by the same token, the first choice is incorrect.

The other "no" answer--"that test obviously has nothing to do with athletic ability"--is incorrect because it is irrelevant. Perhaps the test has no <u>face</u> validity, but it does seem to have criterion-related validity, and the latter is what we are concerned with. (Review frames 15-16 if you gave this answer.)

The final "yes" answer--"the test is a valid test of athletic ability"--is misleading because there is no such thing as a "valid" test <u>in general</u>: it depends on what aspect of validity you are focusing on. However, this point was not stressed in the text and you should consider yourself correct if you gave this answer <u>and</u> the other "yes" answer.

3. False; true; false (frames 29, 32, 33, 36, 38)
4. both of the above (the first two statements) (frames 36, 39)

CHAPTER FIVE

Reliability

1.   <u>Reliability</u> refers to the degree to which a measuring procedure
gives consistent results. In the first example in this book it was pointed out that when we take two different measurements of the same person's height, we would not be at all surprised to get different results
each time.
    You might want to do an experiment yourself to illustrate this
point. Simply measure the width of your desk twice. What would you
expect?

_____   two identical results
_____   two different results with a fairly small discrepancy
_____   two widely discrepant results

- -

probably two different results but with a fairly small discrepancy

2.   If you tried it and got identical results, more power to you! Now
try it a few more times--or try measuring the wall instead of your
desk. Sooner or later you will encounter small discrepancies.
    There are now only two ways to explain this fact. Which one is
more likely?

_____   The actual width of the desk keeps changing.
_____   The measuring procedure is not perfectly reliable.

- -

The measuring procedure is not perfectly reliable.

3.   Reliability is not a serious problem when we measure furniture--
but it can be one when we measure human beings. Consider the following factors:
    (1) When we measure furniture, the difference in results will gen-
erally tend to be small, perhaps a fraction of an inch. But in human
testing, we might get significantly large differences. (Undoubtedly
you've often felt that if you'd just "had a few breaks" you could have
scored 90 instead of 70.)

(2) The decisions to be made when we measure furniture usually
are not too important. Who cares if his desk is 38 or 38.1 inches
wide? But educational and psychological tests often are used in making critical decisions about schooling, employment, or psychiatric
treatment--to mention just a few.

(3) When we use a tape measure, even if the results are not always consistent, we still know from long experience that it is a correct method of measurement. We are not equally certain about every
test we use. Thus a lack of reliability can cast doubt on the merits of
the test itself.

(4) When we measure furniture, even if we are making an import-
ant decision based on a <u>small</u> difference using an <u>unreliable</u> measuring
measuring procedure, we always have the option of taking large numbers of repeated measurements. Through sheer repetition we will be
able to "zero in" on an accurate result. Not so with humans. Although
we can test a person two or even three times on the same test, we
can't do it much more than that. Give a few reasons why:

_____

_____

_____

- -

(Answers are given below.)

4.   Time and cost are two reasons that need not be elaborated. In
addition, there are <u>practice effects</u> from taking a test again. Even if
the right answers are never given to the student, he may get some degree of added proficiency just from taking the test a repeated number
of times. There are also <u>fatigue effects</u>. This phrase does not refer
only to physical tiredness; rather, the "fatigue" effect simply means
that as we take the same test a repeated number of times, we may
tend to do worse because of boredom, lack of motivation, etc.

Realistically, then, our problem is not that we often get two different results. Rather, the problem is that we test only once, but that
we <u>might have obtained</u> a different result under other circumstances.
We never really know.

Just as we have validity studies, however, we also have reliability studies that enable us to estimate the degree of reliability of any
test. For example, consider again our 30 students listed in Exhibit 9.
Suppose we give them the same test--the Hypothetical Test of Intellectual Ability--a few months later. If the test is generally (but not perfectly) reliable, what would we expect?

_____ Everyone would get the identical score the second time.
_____ Most scores would be different, but only by a few points.
_____ The order of the 30 students would be generally the same
        (that is, student #8 would be at the top or close to it, stu-
        dent #11 would be at the bottom or close to it, and so on).

- -

Most scores would be different, but only by a few points.
The order of students would be generally the same.

5.   The only way to find out is to try. So two months later, the same
30 students who took the HTIA in our validity study now take the identical test again as part of a reliability study. The results of this hypothetical study are shown in Exhibit 14 (page 139).

From your inspection of the data in Exhibit 14, would you say that
at least one of the two statements in the preceding answer have been
verified? (YES/NO)

- -

YES (Both turn out to be generally true, as we will see in the next
few frames.)

6.   But, as always we do not trust to simple inspection of the data.
We follow the same procedure as in the validity study. Our task is to
ascertain the <u>correlation</u> between test scores on the first and second
occasions.

First, to get a visual impression of the data, we graph the results.
This has been done in Exhibit 15 (page 140). Looking at this graph,
what is your impression of the correlation between the two sets of test
scores?

      _____ negative correlation
      _____ no correlation
      _____ positive but relatively weak correlation
      _____ positive and relatively strong correlation

If you have any trouble with this question, ask yourself the following:
Which graph on page 78 does Exhibit 15 most resemble?

- -

positive and relatively strong correlation
(It most resembles graph A.)

7.   What we learn from Exhibit 15 (or from the data in Exhibit 14, on
which the graph is based) is that persons who scored high in September
generally scored high in November as well, and that those who scored
low in September generally scored low in November. If this had not
been the case, the graph would not tend to resemble a straight line going from lower left to upper right.

In an earlier example, we graphed the results of the test against
the criterion of academic grade averages. The results were shown in
Exhibit 10. Which of the two graphs indicates a stronger (higher) positive correlation?

_____ Exhibit 10
_____ Exhibit 15

- -

Exhibit 15 (In Exhibit 10 there are more deviations from the straight-line pattern.)

8.   On commonsense grounds, which correlation coefficient would we expect to be higher?

_____ the correlation between test scores and the non-test criterion
_____ the correlation between scores on the test and scores on the same test a few months later

- -

the correlation between scores on the test and scores on the same test a few months later

9.   This is how it turned out, as we have seen in comparing Exhibits 10 and 15. When we design a test that is supposed to correlate with some criterion as evidence of its validity, we expect the relationship to be moderately or fairly strong, but by no means perfect. A validity coefficient of .60 is considered high.
      When we are comparing a test not with some outside criterion but but simply with itself, we would naturally expect the correlation to be much higher. In fact, we start off by assuming that the correlation of a test administered two different times to the same group of people would be perfect. This assumption is unrealistic, of course, because we already know (from Chapter 1 and from common sense) that there are many sources of measurement error.
      Given that reliability coefficients should be higher than validity coefficients, but not absolutely perfect, what kind of correlation should we expect when we do a reliability study?

_____ between .20 and .60
_____ in the .80's or .90's
_____ a perfect correlation: +1.00

- -

in the .80's or .90's

10.   As you looked over the choices you may have noticed that the possibility of a correlation in the .70's was omitted. This is difficult to deal with. As correlation coefficients go, the .70's is generally considered quite high, but it is not high enough for a reliability coefficient. For the HTIA, the correlation coefficient (which we have computed by a formula from the data in Exhibit 14) turns out to be .78.

This is considerably higher than the validity coefficient of .57 (frame 34, page 79), but is still on the low side for a reliability coefficient. After all, we are talking about the same test given under the same conditions to the same students only a few months later. So whenever we want to make use of HTIA results, we have to bear in mind that the results reflect not only "intellectual ability," but also a considerable amount of measurement error.

Up to now we have been using the term "measurement error" to refer to:

  _____   mistakes made in scoring or administering a test
  _____   inevitable differences in results when tests or measurements are taken a second time

- -

inevitable differences in results when tests or measurements are taken a second time

11.   That definition is correct, but now that we are confronted with somewhat less reliability evidence than we would like, we can no longer shrug off the results as simply due to some inevitable and unspecified sources of measurement error. We need to look into the possible reasons for the low reliability correlation.

When we obtained (in our hypothetical experiment) two different results for the width of a desk, we ruled out the possibility that the desk itself had changed. Can we rule out the possibility that the intellectual ability of the students has changed in two months? (YES/NO)

- -

Since a case can be made for either possibility, the correct answer has to be NO--we cannot absolutely rule it out.

12.   Whether the answer is YES or NO, we have problems. Suppose that intellectual ability, as measured by this test, actually does change in a few months. If ability really does change, then a good test (SHOULD/SHOULD NOT) give identical results the second time.

- -

SHOULD NOT

13.   That may be what happened in this case. Maybe we have an extremely good test--so good that it can accurately reflect changes in intellectual ability over a few months.

But there are two problems. First, we know from long experience that basic intellectual ability does not change very much, certainly not at age 13 or 14 and in only two months--especially when all students have been in the same school during those two months.

Second and more important, consider the purpose of the test. It is supposed to be able to predict what kind of courses students will benefit from two or three years later in high school. If intellectual ability itself actually changes in a few months, then the test (CAN/CANNOT) serve this purpose.

- -

CANNOT

14.   So we have two possibilities--that the intellectual ability that this test is designed to measure does not change in just a few months, or the less likely one that it does change, in which case the test cannot possibly serve a useful predictive purpose. In any case, before coming to any conclusions about the test, we have to look for other reasons to explain the relatively low reliability revealed in our experiment.

        We saw in Chapter 1 that fluctuations in mood, physical health, and motivation may affect performance. The more these factors are operating, the (LESS/MORE) consistent the results will be or, in other words, the (LESS/MORE) reliability the test will have.

- -

LESS consistent
LESS reliability

15.   Although fluctuations of this nature are inevitable, they are not desirable. Like most tests, this test is designed to measure a student's ability--not his mood level. Assuming that the basic ability does not change, we want to make our test reliable enough so that it will:

_____   respond to fluctuations in mood, physical factors, etc.; that is, give different results on different occasions
_____   withstand fluctuations in mood, physical factors, etc.; that is, give the same results on different occasions

- -

withstand fluctuations in mood, physical factors, etc.

16.   In order to determine the degree to which this is the case, we have to do an experiment as we have described--that is, give the same test to the same students a second time. This is called a test-retest study, and the resulting correlation coefficient is known as a test-retest coefficient or simply retest reliability.

        Of the three methods that we will discuss for ascertaining the reliability of a test, the test-retest method usually is expected to yield a high reliability coefficient because it is the only method in which we give the identical test to the identical sample of subjects under identical conditions (same place, same person giving the instructions, etc.-- if possible).

The advantages of the test-retest method will be more readily apparent after we have discussed the other methods. The disadvantages, however, are clear. First, as already discussed, we don't know the extent to which the students themselves actually change in ability (we can assume that they don't change, but that doesn't mean that they actually don't). Second, we have the problems of fatigue effects and practice effects. In our example the students took the test in September and then again in November. Which of the following would be plausible fatigue effects?

_____ The students might be physically tired from taking the test twice.
_____ They might be less motivated, particularly if they think that only the first result "counts."
_____ They might be bored and therefore spend less time on the test.

- -

They might be less motivated, particularly if they think that only the first result "counts."
They might be bored and therefore spend less time on the test.
(The first possibility is unlikely. It is doubtful that students would be physically tired as a result of having taken the same test two months ago.)

17. Practice effects could also be present. For example, after the original administration of the test in September, the students might have compared notes. Even if the right answers are not given to them, it would be easy enough for them to ask around and even look up a few things that made them curious.

If there is a general tendency for scores to rise because of practice effects and to fall because of fatigue effects, you might think that they would cancel each other out. But this assumes that practice and fatigue effects are operating with equal force, which is not necessarily the case. And in general, as we noted in frame 43, page 84, any time we induce a situation that affects results and has nothing to do with actual ability, we tend to distort the "true" results that would be achieved if there were no extraneous factors present.

It is important to keep in mind that practice and fatigue effects usually do not present a problem in a normal testing situation--that is, when the test is given only once. The only reason they become a problem is that for research purposes we are giving the same test a second time to the same students. If we could somehow magically do this without any possibility of fatigue or practice effects, then we would expect the results of the second test to be more similar to the results of the first test. In other words, without the artificial problems of practice and fatigue effects, the test-retest reliability coefficient between the September results and the November results would probably have been:

_____ higher than .78
_____ lower than .78
_____ no change

- -

higher than .78 (If you do not fully understand this point, it should become clearer after we have studied other ways of estimating the reliability of a test.)

18.   Suppose, then, that we gave the same students the same <u>kind</u> of test a second time, but with different questions. For example, we would still have, say, 10 vocabulary questions, but the actual words would be different. We would have 10 arithmetic problems, but with different numbers--and so on. Compared to the original method of using the <u>same</u> questions, what would be the result in terms of practice and fatigue effects?

_____ reduction of practice effects
_____ reduction of fatigue effects
_____ both
_____ neither

Explain your answer:

_____

_____

- -

both (Explanation is given below.)

19.   Using the same test with different questions would either eliminate practice effects altogether or reduce them so considerably that we wouldn't have to worry about them. True, some amount of practice is obtained just by being experienced at taking a certain <u>kind</u> of test. This is negligible, however, when compared to the practice effect that results from actually learning some of the right answers. Fatigue effects would also be reduced, if not eliminated, because from the student's point of view the test is a new one that he has not taken before.
    When two test booklets are identical in structure, type of content, length, and other characteristics, but contain different actual questions, they are known as <u>alternate forms</u> of the same test. For example, we might have a vocabulary test in which words are given and the student makes a choice from three definitions. "Form A" of this test would contain 40 such examples; "Form B" would contain 40 <u>different</u> examples of equal difficulty.
    It should be pointed out that the phrase "alternate form" is misleading. What is being changed, as the preceding example indicates, is the (FORM/CONTENT) of the test.

CONTENT   (The phrase "alternate form" actually refers to the printed forms, not to the "form" of the test.)

20.   As already discussed, one reason for using the alternate-form method of estimating reliability, rather than the test-retest method, is that it tends to reduce or eliminate the problem of fatigue and practice effects. This, however, should be considered mainly a side benefit. There is a much more important reason for estimating reliability by the alternate-form method.

Consider the 40 words on the hypothetical vocabulary test mentioned in the preceding frame. It is well known that size of vocabulary is one of the best indicators of verbal ability in general and is highly correlated with many measures of intellectual capacity. The words that you generally see on a vocabulary test, however--"fractious," "hirsute," "rodomontade," and the like--rarely appear in actual speech or writing. Even professional writers seldom use such words, and when they do they will probably first check the meaning in a dictionary.

Given these facts and assumptions, why do we give a 40-word vocabulary test?

_____   The words on the test can be considered a sample that would enable us to estimate the extent of the person's entire vocabulary.

_____   The words on the test are important to know in themselves.

_____   Someone who knows many of those words is likely to be very strong in other intellectual abilities as well.

The words on the test can be considered a sample that would enable us to estimate the extent of the person's entire vocabulary.
Someone who knows many of those words is likely to be very strong in other intellectual abilities as well.

21. Although these two answers express different thoughts, the basic concept is the same: The test is a sample. Whether we are interested in vocabulary itself or vocabulary as a predictor of other abilities, we clearly cannot give every single word in the English language.

The same principle of the test being a sample holds for arithmetic, intelligence, musical abilities, or indeed any test that contains a finite number of items selected from a virtually infinite number of possibilities. For any dimension of interest, we clearly cannot ask every possible question or require the student to perform every possible task.

So the obvious question that arises is: Do we have an adequate sample? This means, at a bare minimum, that it should be of the right size and have the right kinds of items.

Suppose, then, that we give Form A of the vocabulary test to, say, 100 college freshmen. Then we give Form B, containing 40 different words, to the same 100 persons. If both forms contain a good sample of 40 words that adequately reflect general vocabulary, and if the two forms are indeed of equivalent difficulty, what should we expect?

_____ Students who do well on Form A should do equally well on Form B.

_____ The rank order of the 100 students should be highly similar on both forms.

_____ There should be a high positive correlation between the results on Form A and the results on Form B.

_____ Since these are two different tests using different word lists, we would not necessarily expect any correlation between results on Form A and results on Form B.

- -

the fourth statement is incorrect; all the others are correct and represent different ways of saying the same thing.

22.   Given that we would expect a high correlation, how high?

_____ in the .80's or .90's; in other words, as in a good reliability coefficient

_____ between .20 and .60; in other words, as in a good validity coefficient

- -

in the .80's or .90's; in other words, as in a good reliability coefficient

23.   In effect, when we give two alternate forms of the same test, it is somewhat as if we were measuring the same desk with two different tape measures, or even with a tape measure and a wooden yardstick. We expect the results to be quite similar, although probably not identical.

Now suppose that the alternate-form correlation coefficient turned out to be low or moderate, rather than in the .80's or .90's. One of many disturbing possibilities is that the two samples of 40 words each (WERE/WERE NOT) equivalent.

- -

WERE NOT

24.   If this turns out to be the case, we can simply revise the two tests and keep trying them out until we get a high correlation. That, in fact, is one of the purposes of an alternate-form reliability study.

    Suppose, however, that no matter how often we tried, we could not come up with two forms that were genuinely equivalent--that is, we could never obtain sufficiently high correlations between the two forms. What might we conclude?

_____ There is no such thing as "general vocabulary"; a test
        can only measure the degree to which certain people
        happen to know certain words.
_____ There is such a thing as "general vocabulary" which
        can be tested.

_ _

(Answer is discussed below.)

25.   In the hypothetical circumstances that we have outlined, we would have to conclude that there really is no such thing as "general vocabulary," or if so that we cannot sample it with a test. Actually, in the real world, this is no problem with vocabulary tests. But it may well be a problem with other tests in which the abilities themselves are not so easily definable or well researched as vocabulary.

    Thus another advantage of an alternate-form reliability study is that it serves as an indicator of whether or not the test is actually measuring some specific ability that really is worth postulating as an entity--rather than general intellectual ability or good skills at test-taking.

    In review from our discussion in Chapter 4, this is another way of asking whether or not the test has:

_____ criterion-related validity
_____ construct validity
_____ both

_ _

construct validity

26.   Another aspect of validity that we mentioned in Chapter 4 is content validity. This refers to the question of whether the sample of items in the test is truly the most genuinely representative sample of all possible items that could be on the test (as discussed in frame 21 of this chapter).

    Alternate-form reliability enables us to check on both the construct and content validity of a test. Suppose we obtained a very low alternate-form reliability coefficient. That means, as already discussed, that the two tests werenot really equivalent. Another way to look at this is to say that since the two forms are not really equivalent, one is probably a "better" test than the other in that questions have been chosen more wisely. This problem has to do with (CONTENT/CONSTRUCT) validity.

CONTENT (Construct validity deals with whether or not the ability really exists; content validity deals with whether or not the test questions are the best ones to measure that ability if it does exist.)

27.   Summarizing thus far, the purpose of a reliability coefficient is to indicate the degree to which test results will be consistent. When we use the alternate-form method, however, we do several other things. We can get at least a gross check on construct and content validity. And since the two forms are usually administered on two separate occasions, we also get an idea of how mood and similar factors affect results.

This versatility can be a disadvantage, however, in that we don't know, at least from one single study, whether variance in results is due to differences in the two forms of the tests, differences in how the subjects are feeling on two different occasions, or factors having to do with the validity of the test itself.

In fact, the fundamental problem in all reliability studies is exactly this: to sort out the various sources of measurement error. It is a problem, however, that concerns theoreticians and those who actually construct standardized tests. What we need be concerned about is that all these factors may play a part in affecting results.

Another fact to keep in mind, though not actually a disadvantage, is that with the alternate-form method we are not using the identical test twice. This reduces practice and fatigue effects, but in general these effects are less significant than the difference between two forms. Thus, compared to the test-retest method, we will probably tend to get (HIGHER/LOWER) correlation coefficients when we use the alternate-form method.

LOWER

28.   There are, in addition, some practical disadvantages in doing an alternate-form reliability study. First, you have to construct an alternate form. Second, as in a test-retest study, you have to use the same sample of subjects twice. All this takes time and money.

Suppose, then, that we have an arithmetic test of 40 items and we want to estimate its reliability without the practical inconveniences of the alternate-form method. Instead of constructing 40 additional comparable items, let's mentally consider our test to be two tests: one consisting of items 1 through 20 and the other consisting of items 21 through 40. To do this we have to make three important assumptions:

(1) The items in 1-20 are comparable to items 21-40 (although of course the actual examples are different).
(2) There are no fatigue or practice effects as the students reach the end of the test.
(3) Time limit is not involved so that the student can spend ample time on all questions.

If these assumptions are correct, and we split our test into these two equal halves (1 through 20 and 21 through 40), what do we have?

_____ two identical tests
_____ two alternate forms of the same test
_____ two completely different tests that require different abilities

- -

two alternate forms of the same test

29.   Now consider any student--say Peggy Jones. If she gets 18 out of the first 20 correct, and if the three assumptions in frame 28 are correct, how many correct answers would you expect her to get out of the last 20?

_____ 18, or close to it
_____ no way of predicting

- -

18, or close to it

30.   The same would be true, of course, for all students. Our results might turn out somewhat as follows:

Student	First half	Second half
Peggy	18	17
Arthur	13	14
Louise	10	10
Carla	19	20
. . .	. . .	. . .

This is one type of a split-half method of estimating reliability. As the table indicates, we would expect to get a (HIGH/LOW/MODERATE) correlation between results on the two halves.

- -

HIGH (Those who score high on one half also score high on the other half.)

31.   In general, "split-half" refers to any method of dividing one test into equivalent forms. The top-bottom method, which we have described, is rarely used in practice, for it requires the assumptions (as mentioned in frame 28) that students have ample time to devote to all items and that their performance will neither improve nor deteriorate as they proceed to the bottom. What is usually done, therefore, is to consider the odd-numbered and the even-numbered items as two alternate forms.

In an "odd-even" reliability study, the student takes the test only once. Each student gets two scores--one for the total number of odd-numbered items answered correctly, and one for the correct even-numbered items. The results are tabulated exactly as in frame 30, except that the heading "first half" is changed to "_____," and the heading "second half" is changed to "_____."

- - - - - - - - - - - - - - - - - - - -

"odd-numbered items"
"even-numbered items"
(or equivalent words, in either order)

32.   We have, then, the same situation as in the vocabulary tests, where we used Form A and Form B. We are doing the same thing here, but we are not labeling the two halves as such and we are administering both "forms" (halves) at a single sitting.
      The only disadvantage here is that each of the two halves is, of course, shorter than the test as a whole. In general, other factors being equal, the more items on a test, the more reliable it is. Thus, either one of the two subtests would actually be (MORE/LESS) reliable than the complete test.

- - - - - - - - - - - - - - - - - - - -

LESS

33.   Suppose, for example, that the correlation coefficient between the odd-numbered and even-numbered items turned out to be .82. For such a cut-and-dried affair as an arithmetic test this would seem quite disappointing. However, when we consider that each test contains only 20 items, it isn't bad at all. Our question, though, is what would happen if we had constructed an alternate form of all 40 items? From the data given, and a formula known as the Spearman-Brown Prophecy Formula, we could estimate that the reliability of the complete 40-item test is not .82, but actually a very respectable .90. Another formula, Kuder-Richardson Formula #21, gives essentially the same result as the Spearman-Brown formula.
      It is not important to remember these names or to know how to use the formulas, but you will run across them in test manuals and in virtually every article you read that has to do with reliability. For example, suppose you read the following comment about an existing test:

      "Split-half reliability is .85 (KR #21)."

      The parenthetical remark indicates that Kuder-Richardson Formula #21 has been used to give a corrected correlation coefficient. In other words, the reliability of .85 is:

_____ the correlation coefficient actually obtained when results of one half were compared with results on the other half
_____ the estimated reliability coefficient of the entire test

_ _

the estimated reliability coefficient of the entire test

34.   The main advantage of the odd-even (or any other split-half) method is that the reliability study can be undertaken at one sitting. This
is obviously advantageous in terms of time and cost, and also in terms
of eliminating the problem of practice or fatigue effects. Moreover,
since the students take the test only once, we do not introduce additional sources of measurement error through changes in how they feel
on different occasions.
      Yet this same advantage is also a disadvantage, for we usually
want to know whether or not a test is reliable enough to give similar
results on different occasions, notwithstanding the different moods and
feelings of the persons who take it, or other extraneous features such
as a noisy room. If we were interested only in this question, which
method would we use ?

_____ test-retest method
_____ alternate-form method
_____ split-half method

_ _

test-retest method

35.   In review, there are three basic methods for determining reliability, as listed below. (The order has no significance.) Give a brief
description of each and mention the main problem or disadvantage
(other than time and cost) associated with each.

SUMMARY OF METHODS FOR ESTIMATING RELIABILITY

Test-Retest Method:

_____

_____

_____

_____

Alternate-Form Method:

_____

_____

_____

_____

Split-Half Method:

_____

_____

_____

_____

- -

Test-Retest Method: The identical test is given to the same group of persons on two different occasions. Problems: Practice or fatigue effects may reduce the reliability coefficient; students might change in ability (depending on the time interval and the kind of ability being tested).

Alternate-Form Method: Two different forms of the same test are given to the same persons on different occasions. The questions on each form are equivalent but different. Problems: It is not always easy to construct equivalent forms; many different variables come into play (see frame 27).

Split-Half Method: Test is scored as two equivalent subtests consisting of odd-numbered and even-numbered items (or some other basis of splitting). Problem: It does not take into account the effects of testing on a different occasion.

Consider yourself correct if you mentioned one of the other problems that was covered in the test, or even if you simply had the general idea behind each method. In practice your task will be to recognize the meaning of these terms when you see them, rather than to define them.

36.   Before a standardized test is published, the author will often use all three methods to assess the reliability of the test. When you read about a test in a manual or an article, you may well see three different reliability coefficients. Unfortunately, there is no general way of stating which of the many possible reliability coefficients should be taken as "the" reliability figure. This depends on the purpose for which the test will be used and many other factors.

To illustrate one of the important uses of a reliability coefficient, however, we have to assume that reliability is represented by one and only one number, such as .83 or .91. So in the remainder of this book we will talk about "the reliability coefficient" without specifying how it was derived.

In this next chapter we will show how the reliability coefficient can be used to determine the amount of measurement error that might be expected on a test result.

(No answer necessary.)

TEST FOR CHAPTER 5

1. Briefly describe each of the methods for estimating the reliability
    of a test. (It is not necessary to give advantages and disadvant-
    ages.)

    Split-Half: _____

                        _____

    Test-Retest: _____

                        _____

    Alternate-Form: _____

                        _____

2. In practice, the best way to ascertain "split-half" reliability is to
    divide the test into two equal parts according to which method ?

    _____ top-bottom
    _____ odd-even

3. A test of mathematical ability has a split-half reliability of .84
    and a test-retest reliability of .89. An alternate form for the test
    is devised. The two forms--call tham A, the original form, and
    B, the alternate form--are given to the same sample of subjects
    at a one-week interval. The correlation coefficient between the
    Form A results and the Form B results is .65.
    (a) As a first reaction, what do you think of this result?
         _____ surprisingly high
         _____ surprisingly low
         _____ about as expected

    (b) What is the most likely explanation for the result?

         _____ practice and fatigue effects
         _____ the two forms were not really comparable
         _____ the original test (Form A) is an unreliable test
         _____ the actual mathematical ability of the students
                 has changed

4. Suppose you have a "Scientific Aptitude Test" of 60 items. You
    want to get an idea of the test's reliability and its content validity.
    You have the time and funds to do one study, but only one. What
    would you do ?

    _____ split-half
    _____ test-retest
    _____ alternate-form

5. Content validity refers to the questions of whether:

    _____ The test is an adequate sample of all the items that con-
            ceivably could have been on it.
    _____ The test is measuring some specific ability rather than
            general intelligence or some other general ability.

_____ The test can predict how well people will do in terms of performance on a meaningful criterion.

6. A test author claims that his test is quite reliable in that it will give essentially the same results no matter how students are feeling on the particular day they take it. What kind of reliability evidence would best support this claim?

_____ test-retest
_____ alternate-form
_____ split-half

7. Students take a multiple-choice examination in American History. They are not told the correct answers. A week later they take the identical test. The correlation coefficient between the two sets of test results is .85.
(a) What kinds of effects might have been a factor?

_____ practice effects
_____ fatigue effects
_____ both

Explain your answer: _____

_____

(b) No matter what you gave as your answer, if these effects had not been operating, the correlation coefficient would probably have been:

_____ higher than .85
_____ lower than .85

Answers

1. Split-Half: The test is divided into two equivalent halves. Each half is scored separately. (If you described the odd-even method, consider yourself correct since that is almost always used.)
Test-Retest: The same test is given to the same persons on a second occasion.
Alternate-Form: Two different forms of the same test are given to the same persons.
(frame 35)

2. odd-even (frame 33, also 28)

3. (a) Surprisingly low. Reliability coefficients are usually higher than the .60's, and we have already obtained two reliability coefficients in the .80's for this test. (If you answered "about as expected," see frames 22-23.)
(b) The two forms were not really comparable. It is doubtful if mathematical ability changes in a week, the original test was shown to be reliable as stated in the question, and practice and fatigue effects are small compared to a possible incomparability of forms. (frame 27; see frames 22-27 if you missed both parts of this question)

4. Alternate-form. The split-half method is similar, but since you have the time and funds you might as well take advantage of them and use two 60-item tests rather than two 30-item subtests. (frames 26-27)

5. The test is an adequate sample of all the items that conceivably could have been on it. (frames 20-21)

6. test-retest (frames 14-16)

7. (a) Both. They might have learned some of the correct answers on their own (practice effect) and/or have been uninterested or less motivated to do well (fatigue effect).
    (b) higher than .85. (frames 16-17)

CHAPTER SIX
Standard Error of Measurement

1. In connection with every test discussed so far, real and hypothetical, we have mentioned that a particular score a person gets should be considered as:

    _____ the absolute value that definitively measures his ability

    _____ a number that indicates a probable range of scores that he might have attained

- -

a number that indicates a probable range of scores that he might have attained

2. For example, if Nathan's IQ score turns out to be 114 on one occasion, for all we know his "true" IQ score may be 123 or 105 (or anywhere in between, or even higher or lower than those limits). The difference, of course, is considerable--especially if we are using arbitrary cut-off points to label a child (an erroneous practice at best) or to decide which section of a divided classroom he will go into.

Even in sticking to a straight statistical interpretation, the difference between an IQ of 105 and 123 may give us an entirely different picture of the child. As review, convert IQ's of 105 and 123 into percentile equivalents, assuming that they are deviation IQ's with mean 100 and SD = 16. You may refer to any part of this book to refresh your memory.

- -

105: 62nd percentile
123: 92nd percentile
(If you had trouble, review frame 10 on page 47 or the test to Chapter 3 on page 65.)

3.   Since results of different measurements always tend to vary, theoretically the only way we can ascertain the "true" single number-- whether we are measuring a desk or testing a person--is to perform the measuring procedure (e.g., give the test) an <u>infinite</u> number of times and average the results. In practice we have to use statistical techniques for estimating the probable range of values that is indicated by one given score. Does 116 mean that the true IQ is somewhere be- tween 100 and 132? 114 and 118? In part the answer depends on how high a <u>level of confidence</u> we require, and in part on a computation of the <u>standard error of measurement</u> for the test in question.

To illustrate the related concepts "standard error of measure- ment" and "confidence level," let's return to our problem of measur- ing a desk. You obtain a result of 37 7/8 inches. Your friend claims that you're off by at least an inch. So you measure again, and this time you get a result of 38 1/8 inches. You now say that you've re- vised your estimate to 38.0 inches (averaging the two) but your friend still says you're off by an inch or more.

There is only one way to put a stop to this kind of harassment, and that is with a gentlemanly wager. It is agreed between you that a third party will be called in to measure the desk with the same tape measure a dozen times and that you will accept the mean of these dozen results as the true value.

You say the desk is 38 inches wide. Your friend is willing to bet that it is less than 37 inches <u>or</u> more than 39 inches wide. Assuming he has no tricks up his sleeve, how certain are you that the true value will fall between 37 and 39 inches?

_____ absolutely (100 percent) certain
_____ very, very sure
_____ quite sure
_____ about 50 percent sure
_____ in great doubt

(If you didn't answer 100 percent or 50 percent, try putting a number next to your answer.)

- -

If you said 100 percent, you'll probably be right this time, but you may lose a lot of money one of these days. If you said less than 98 percent, you may be just a wee bit timid.

4.   Just before the bet is made, your friend says he's changed his mind--now he thinks you're off by <u>half</u> an inch or more. (He had previously said you were off by at least an inch.) Now how certain are you that you are right that he is wrong? _____ percent.

- -

Your confidence level should be somewhat smaller, but still high in the 90-100 percent range. After all, how frequently are you off by half an inch when you measure a desk?

5.   If your friend keeps hedging and narrowing the limits--1/4 of an inch, 1/8 of an inch, and so on--your confidence will gradually decrease until it is only a 50-50 proposition, or possibly even less. On the other hand, if he expands the limits--that is, claims that you are off by two, three, or even more inches than that--your confidence will approach 100 percent certainty, or close enough to it so that you are ready to go out and pawn the family jewels to raise cash for the bet.

We have, then, two elements to consider: your confidence level, and what you conceive to be the "standard error of measurement" for measuring a desk of this size with your tape measure. Through experience you know that if different measurements that you take are all within a range of, say, 1/4 of an inch, then any given measurement is likely to be "off" by about 1/8 or 1/16 of an inch, or somewhere in that vicinity--certainly not half an inch.

These same elements enter into the interpretation of test results, but we cannot rely on "instinct." We need quantitative information. The first thing we want to know is: To what extent does this test give consistent results? To answer this we need to know a correlation coefficient that measures the test's (RELIABILITY/VALIDITY).

- -

RELIABILITY (if incorrect, see frame 1, page 92)

6.   But even a highly reliable test is subject to a certain degree of variation. What is the numerical quantity that is used as a measure of variability?

        _____ mean
        _____ median
        _____ standard deviation
        _____ percentile

- -

standard deviation

7.   When we make a bet about the measurement of a desk, we have "in our head" some conception of the reliability of our tape measure--extremely high, though not absolutely perfect. We also have "in our head" an idea of the standard deviation that we might obtain if we actually computed it on the basis of many measurements. With a test, we have no way of knowing all this information on our own, but it will be provided by the publisher in the test manual.

Given the test's reliability coefficient and standard deviation, we can compute the standard error of measurement--that is, the extent to which we expect that a single obtained result might differ from the "true" result that we would obtain if we tested the person an infinite number of times.

The formula is:

$$SEM = s\sqrt{1 - r}$$

where SEM stands for the standard error of measurement, r stands for the reliability coefficient, and s stands for the standard deviation.

We'll apply this formula to the problem of determining Nathan's "true" IQ score (frame 2). First we need to know the reliability of the particular intelligence test in question. As stated earlier, there is no such thing as "the" reliability--there are many different methods. To illustrate how the formula works, let's assume that the reliability coefficient, r, is .91. Thus 1 - r = 1 - .91, or .09. The square root of .09 is .3.

Now we need to know the standard deviation. Since the score is in deviation IQ units, the standard deviation is 16.

Given all the formula and these information, what is the standard error of measurement (SEM)? _____

- -

SEM = 4.8 (16 x .3)

8.   In Chapter 2 we stated that 68 percent of all scores fall within one standard deviation of the mean, 95 percent of all scores fall within two standard deviations of the mean, and that virtually all scores fall within three standard deviations of the mean.

The relationship between the true value and the standard error of measurement is the same as the relationship between the mean and the standard deviation. (This is not a coincidence; both have to do with properties of the normal distribution.) In other words, there is a 68 percent probability that a person's true score will be within one standard error of measurement (in either direction) from his obtained score.*

Nathan's obtained score, in IQ terms, was 114. The standard error of measurement has been computed to be 4.8, which for convenience we'll round up to 5.0. This means that there is a 68 percent chance that his "true" IQ is somewhere between 109 and _____.

- -

119 (Caution: Do not make a practice of rounding the SEM; we are doing it only in this introductory example.)

---

*Note: This statement is not absolutely accurate in theory, but close enough to accuracy in practice.

9.   This is by no means an uncomfortably large range. Now that we know the standard error of measurement, and given the many precautions against the misuse of labels, we could label this result as "high average" or something to that effect, not really caring whether his "true" IQ score is 110, 118, 111, 117, or whatever.

We could do so only with 68 percent confidence, however, because only 68 percent of all scores are within one SEM of the "true" score. That means that there is only a 2-to-1 chance (approximately) that we are correct in assuming that Nathan's "true" score actually is in this range. If we used the same confidence level (68 percent) with all 32 children in a classroom, we would be wrong in regard to 10 of them.

You wouldn't go pawn the family jewels to bet against your friend unless you were, say, at least 95 percent certain. This might mean that you would require a "safety range" of at least an inch (depending on the answers you gave a few frames back). Similarly, in the field of tests and measurements we like to be 95 percent certain of practically anything, even if we have to stretch our "safety range" by many more points.

In other words, we would prefer to extend the probable limits of the true score to <u>two</u> standard errors of measurement away from the observed score. This would give us 95 percent certainty.

In this example the standard error of measurement has been computed to be 4.8; twice this amount = 9.6. Nathan's IQ score was 114. We could say with 95 percent certainty that his "true" IQ score (on this particular test) is 114 $\pm$ (plus or minus) 9.6, or somewhere between _____ and _____

- -

104.4 (114 - 9.6) and 123.6 (114 + 9.6)

10.   Converting these limits into z scores and percentile ranks,

$$\frac{104.4 - 100}{16} = \frac{4.4}{16} = .3; \quad PR = 62$$

and

$$\frac{123.6 - 100}{16} = \frac{23.6}{16} = 1.5; \quad PR = 93$$

Thus, if we want to be 95 percent certain about Nathan on the basis of his one IQ score of 114 obtained on one test, we would have to say that he might be somewhat above average (62nd percentile) or, on the other hand, that his "true" IQ might be as high as 124, which might well make him the "brightest" child in his classroom (as measured by this test)!

We will discuss the implications of this after some brief review of the standard error of measurement. If you want to skip the review, turn now to frame 16.

(<u>No answer necessary.</u>)

11.   OPTIONAL PRACTICE EXERCISE #1

Suppose that on a certain test the standard error of measurement, computed by the formula in frame 7, turns out to be 4 points (in terms of raw score points). Ron's raw score on the test was 53. We could be 68 percent certain that his "true" score on this test is somewhere between _____ and _____. To be 95 percent certain, we would have to multiply the SEM by 2. In that case, his "true" score would be in a range somewhere between _____ and _____.

- -

68% confidence: between 49 and 57
95% confidence: between 45 and 61

12.   We usually want to have a confidence level of 95 percent, which means that the SEM must be multiplied by 2. If we desire, however, we can choose any confidence level. If you have had a statistics course you will recognize this as a classic "confidence-limits" problem. (If you have not had such a course, or if you would prefer to forget all about it, skip now to the next frame.)

To ascertain the confidence interval at any level of probability, look up a normal curve table (two-tail) for that percentage. Multiply the SEM by the z entry in the table. Subtract the result from the observed score to get the lower confidence limit (exactly as we did in the previous frame).

As you may recall from your statistics course, z for 95 percent is not exactly 2, but 1.96. So when you multiply the SEM by 2 you will be increasing your confidence level to slightly above 95 percent--not that this difference really matters.

If you are interested only in the upper confidence limit (e.g., "I want to be 95 percent certain that George's 'true' IQ is not above 120") or only in the lower confidence limit, use a one-tailed table.

(No answer necessary.)

13.   OPTIONAL PRACTICE EXERCISE #2

The standard deviation of a test is 4 points. The test's reliability is .87. What is the standard error of measurement, using the formula:

$$SEM = s\sqrt{1 - r}$$

(You will need the square root of .13, which is .36.)

SEM = _____

- -

SEM = 1.44   (4 x .36)

14.   CONTINUATION OF PRACTICE EXERCISE 2

On this same test, Henry's raw score was 56. We can be 95 percent certain that his "true" score is within _____ points of this figure
or, in other words, between _____ and _____.

- -

2.88 (using 2 as the multiplier for a 95% confidence level)
53.12 and 58.88 (or 53 and 59--see note below)

15.   A NOTE ON ROUNDING

Since the original raw score was reported as a whole number,
the raw-score confidence limits should also be expressed as whole
numbers, or 53 and 59 in this example. The same result would have
been achieved by rounding 2.88 up to 3. In general, however, it is
advisable not to round during computations, but to do all rounding at
the end. A little bit of rounding at the beginning of a computation can
make a lot of difference at the end.

(No answer necessary.)

16.   Throughout this chapter we have been referring to the "true"
score on a given test (or the "true" value of any measurement.)
What is the "true" score?

_____

Why is it in quotes?

_____

- -

(Answer is given below.)

17.   The "true" score is the score that a person would obtain if he were
tested an infinite number of times and the results averaged. This is a
hypothetical concept (and therefore in quotes) for several reasons. Obviously we cannot test a person an infinite number of times. Even if
we could test a person a large number of times--say, half a dozen--
we should not average the results, because the test would be taken under different conditions each time, there would be practice and fatigue
effects, and the person's actual ability level may have changed. (You
were not expected to mention all this in your answer!)

However, when a teacher, parent, college-admissions officer,
employer, guidance counselor, or the person tested receives a report
of a test score, inevitably he thinks of it as if it were the "true" value.

Nobody really takes the trouble to compute the standard error of measurement and a 95 percent confidence interval. And what do you do with an interval anyway? Moreover, nobody (unless actually making a bet) really distinguishes between 68 percent confidence, 95 percent confidence, and 99 percent confidence. We act as if we had 100 percent confidence.

There is, however, some justification for this situation. If you had to pick one score that you think is most likely to be the "true" score, you might as well pick the observed score (the score the student actually got). It is as good a guess as any, and probably better than most.

In addition, and more fundamentally, statistical decisions that are made on the basis of tests are made on a long-run basis. This is, we know we will have to make some wrong decisions in individual cases, but we also will be right a large percentage of the time. All of the statistical concepts introduced in this book--standard deviation, normal distribution, correlation coefficient, standard error of measurement, and so on--are meaningful only when we consider the individual as part of a large reference population.

We have not gotten into the question of decision-making, since it requires extensive use of statistical concepts and a consideration of many moral and political questions. The example beginning in the next frame (although grossly oversimplified) may give some idea of what is involved, and will also serve to review some of the basic concepts in this book.

(No answer necessary.)

18.   Suppose that at prestigious (and fictitious) Radnoke College, one more place is open in the entering class, and the choice is narrowed down to two applicants--Judy and Irene. In the eyes of the admissions committee, they are equally bright, talented, studious, outgoing, etc. (or whatever the committee likes that particular year). High-school records are equal--in fact everything is equal except morning College Board scores.

On the mathematics section of the SAT, both score 720; on the verbal section, Judy scores 712 and Irene scores 692. How significant is this difference? Should we use it as a basis for making our decision, or should we flip a coin?

First let's ask how significant the test itself is. The basis purpose of the Scholastic Aptitude Test, as used by colleges, is to predict level of accomplishment as measured by grades. How well does it actually do so? This is primarily a question of (VALIDITY/RELIABILITY).

- -

VALIDITY

19.   What kind of validity ?

_____ criterion-related
_____ content
_____ construct

- -

criterion-related

20.   But what criterion? Is the college interested in how well they will
do only in language subjects ? Liberal arts subjects? All subjects?
Suppose both Judy and Irene intend to major in nuclear physics--how
much attention should we pay to their SAT verbal scores ?
        We'll keep it simple and assume that neither Judy nor Irene has
decided on a major, and that the college is interested in how they will
do in all subjects.
        What we need, then, is evidence of criterion-related validity--
that is, a correlation coefficient that expresses the relationship between SAT (verbal) scores and grade averages for women at this type
of college, with mathematical ability and other factors held constant.
        Such a study may actually have been undertaken. (The Educational
Testing Service provides a complete list of publications and research
reports to interested parties.) But since this is a fictitious example,
let us simply assume that the correlation coefficient is .20. This
would actually be a high correlation for the conditions stated above.
(We would expect a higher correlation if we were only predicting grades
in English and if we were talking about the general population rather
than just applicants to schools like Radnoke.)
        Since the correlation coefficient is positive, the person who scores
higher on the test is more likely to get better grades. But how much
more likely? This is answered in Exhibit 16 on page 141.
        Next to the validity correlation coefficient of .20, we see the num-
ber 56. This means that if we made 100 predictions as to who would
get better grades--that is, 100 pairs of Judys and Irenes, year after
year--we would be right _____ times and wrong _____ times.
        If we ignored the test and simply flipped a coin, we would be right
_____ times and wrong _____ times.

- -

Using the test as a predictor of grades: 56 right, 44 wrong
Flipping a coin: 50 right, 50 wrong

        Although these figures indicate that using the test does not greatly
improve decision-making, it must be kept in mind that this is an extreme example in which all other factors have been held constant. In
real life this is rarely the case--there are usually many other aids to
decision-making besides the SAT scores. The test was not designed
to be used as the sole selection instrument.

21.   Now let's turn to the scores themselves. Judy scored 712 and
Irene scored 692. That was certainly a very important Saturday
morning to both of them. Would they have done the same on a different Saturday morning? To answer this we are primarily interested in
knowing the test's _____.

- -

reliability

22.   But what kind of reliability? Our question concerned how they
both happened to feel this particular Saturday morning. The type of
reliability coefficient that would interest us therefore would be:

        _____ test-retest
        _____ alternate-form
        _____ split-half

- -

test-retest

23.   One advantage of using standardized tests is that the test is "the
same for everyone." But is it? The actual test booklet that Judy re-
ceived in Dayton on November 13 probably did not contain the same
questions that Irene had to answer in Chicago on December 4. How
comparable are these results? Now we need to know the correlation
coefficient for:

        _____ test-retest reliability
        _____ alternate-form reliability
        _____ split-half reliability

- -

alternate-form reliability

24.   Given all these reliability factors, what is the probability that
Judy's "true" score could actually be below Irene's? This question
can be answered directly by a statistical formula, but we will go the
long way round and compute the standard error of measurement and
a 95 percent confidence interval.
        We need to work with one reliability coefficient. Let's assume it's
.91--quite high considering that we have both alternate-form and test-
retest factors to consider. In order to compute the standard error of
measurement for this test, we also need to know the test's standard
deviation. In review from Chapter 2, what is the standard deviation
of College Board scores? _____

- -

100

25.   Compute the standard error of measurement using the data in the preceding frame and the formula in frame 7. (The square root that you will need is .3.)

SEM = _____

----

30 points
SEM = $100\sqrt{1 - r}$
      = $100\sqrt{.09}$
      = 100 x .3
      = 30

(If you were incorrect and skipped the optional practice exercises, you should do frames 11-15, beginning on page 116.)

26.   If we want to be 95 percent certain of a range within which the "true" value falls, we have to multiply the standard error of measurement by 2; then add and subtract. Thus if we want to be 95 percent certain about Judy's score, we have to say that it is 712 $\pm$ 60, or between 652 and _____. Irene's result of 692 tells us that her "true" score may be between _____ and _____.

Judy: 652 and 772
Irene: 632 and 752

27.   Radnoke's admissions officer is undoubtedly knowledgeable about measurement error--but what is she to do? Assuming all other factors are equal, she might as well select the applicant with the higher observed score, even though the possibility exists that she is rejecting an applicant (Irene) whose "true" score is as high as 752, in order to admit one whose "true" score may be as low as 652.
        And no matter whose "true" score is higher, that person is only slightly more likely actually to achieve higher grades (see frame 20). The magnitude of the predicted difference is probably quite small, anyway (e.g., 3.2 versus 3.1, or something to that effect). Moreover, grades alone do not indicate much about what a college does for a student or what a student does for a college.
        We see, then, that there are many steps along the way at which wrong decisions can be made, or right decisions for the wrong reasons. If you wanted to change the system, what aspect of it would you focus on?

_____ Admissions officers--they need more training in
        tests and measurements.
_____ The test itself--a better test is needed to measure
        scholastic aptitude.
_____ The criterion--colleges should be less interested in
        who is going to get better grades.

_____ Admissions policies in general--why shouldn't a college want to have a broader spread of ability, rather than trying to get only a narrow range at the top?

_____ Prestige attached to certain colleges--does it really make that much difference whether Irene goes to Radnoke or to Siwash?

_____ The system--every community should have a high-quality college, making competition for places unnecessary.

-- -- -- -- -- -- -- -- -- -- --

(Answer is discussed below.)

28.   There are no objectively "right" answers, but there are some illogical ones--the first two. Better training will not solve any of the problems discussed in this example. Many colleges do have an Office of Tests and Measurements, or some such bureau, staffed by top-notch professionals. More to the point, both the trained person and the untrained person will have to make the same decision anyway--that is, to consider the observed score as the single best estimate of the "true" score.

If you checked any of the last four, then it is quite inconsistent also to check "the test itself." Clearly the test is only a mechanical means to achieving certain ends.

Moreover, since we have had so much to say about the Scholastic Aptitude Test, it is only fair to point out that this particular test stands in very high repute on technical grounds. It has been the subject of hundreds of validity and reliability studies, some undertaken by the publisher and some by outside experts. No one has seriously proposed that any other objective test could do a better job of what the SAT is designed to do.

Incidentally, the standard error of measurement of 30 points may look extremely high, but it isn't. The 30-point figure SEM (assuming a reliability of .91) is based on a scale of 200 to 800, with mean 500 and SD 100. Thirty points on this scale is equivalent to five points on a 0-100 scale.

(No answer necessary.)

29.   So we end where the Preface began--with many social and philosophical questions in which test results themselves play only a small part. In the lives of individuals, however, test results often play a large part. Who should make the final decisions on what kinds of tests there should be and what use should be made of test results? Undoubtedly it would have to be some blend of experts in tests and measurements, political leaders guided by experts, and the public at large--which might include persons who actually take tests.

The Final Examination that begins on page 155 reviews the basic concepts in this book, and also may give you an idea of the kind of analysis that is necessary to tackle some of the broader questions involving tests.   If you do well on it you are not necessarily an expert, but you should be in a good position to read--and perhaps criticize-- what the experts have to say.

(No answer necessary.)

TEST FOR CHAPTER 6

1.   What is meant by a person's "true" score on a test?

_____

_____

2.   Numerically, "measurement error" is:

_____ the difference between a person's "true" score and his score on one given occasion

_____ the number of points a person loses because of mistakes that are his own fault

_____ the probable amount of points lost or gained because of a mistake made in scoring or administering the test

3.   In interpreting a test score we generally think of the score as being within a range of probable values that would include the "true" score, and we generally want to be _____ percent confident that the true score is actually in this range.   (68, 80, 90, 95, or 100 ?)

4.   The mean IQ on the Wechsler Intelligence Scale for Children is 100.   The standard deviation is 15.   There are many different figures for reliability, but for this example say it is .84.

(a) Using the formula SEM $= s\sqrt{1 - r}$, compute the standard error of measurement for this test. (The square root that you will need is either .3, .4, or .5--you should have no trouble guessing which.)

SEM $=$ _____

(b) Which information in the first paragraph was not necessary?

_____ the mean
_____ the standard deviation
_____ the reliability coefficient

(c) Lenore's score on this test is 94 (deviation IQ).   We can be 95 percent certain that her "true" score lies somewhere between:

_____ 88 and 100
_____ 82 and 106
_____ 76 and 112

5.   From a table not in this book, we can determine that in order to be 99 percent certain of the range in which Lenore's "true" score falls, we would have to multiply the SEM by 2.6 (approximately). This comes out to 15.6, which for convenience we'll round up to 16. At this level of confidence (99 percent), we would say that Lenore's "true" score is somewhere between _____ and _____. (Her actual score was 94.)

6.   On being informed of Lenore's score of 94, a common first reaction might be to think of it as "slightly below average." What are some implications of the standard error of measurement (as computed in the above questions) for this type of thinking?

_____

_____

_____

Answers

1.   The average score that would result if the person were tested an infinite number of times. (frames 3, 7)

2.   the difference between a person's "true" score and his score on one given occasion (If you answered either of the others, see frames 3-5, pages 2-3.)

3.   95 percent (frame 9)

4.   (a) $SEM = s\sqrt{1-r}$
$$= 15\sqrt{.16} \quad \text{(r was given as .84)}$$
$$= 15 \times .4$$
$$= 6$$

       (b) not necessary to know the mean

       (c) 82 and 106 (to be 95 percent confident we multiply the SEM by 2)

    (If you missed any of these, see frames 7-12 and do the practice exercises in frames 13-15.)

5.   78 and 110 (16 is subtracted from and added to the score--see frames 9-15)

6.   Her "true" score might actually be well below average or somewhat above average.

or

If she had taken the test on another day her score might have been considerably lower or higher.

or

Because of measurement error, we must be wary of verbal labels. (frames 9-10, 17, 24-27)

Appendix

Exhibits

T Scores

Glossary

Suggestions for Additional Reading

Final Examination

Exhibits

Exhibit 1

Age and Grade Equivalents for Lorge-Thorndike Intelligence Test,
Multilevel Verbal Form 1, Level A

Raw Score	Equiv. Age	Grade	Raw Score	Equiv. Age	Grade	Raw Score	Equiv. Age	Grade	Raw Score	Equiv. Age	Grade
1	6-1	—	26	7-11	2.6	51	9-1	3.8	76	10-8	5.5
2	6-2	—	27	7-11	2.7	52	9-2	3.9	77	10-10	5.6
3	6-4	—	28	8-0	2.7	53	9-2	3.9	78	10-11	5.7
4	6-5	—	29	8-0	2.8	54	9-3	4.0	79	11-0	5.8
5	6-6	—	30	8-1	2.8	55	9-4	4.0	80	11-2	5.9
6	6-7	—	31	8-1	2.9	56	9-4	4.1	81	11-3	6.0
7	6-8	—	32	8-2	2.9	57	9-5	4.1	82	11-5	6.1
8	6-9	—	33	8-3	3.0	58	9-6	4.2	83	11-6	6.2
9	6-10	—	34	8-3	3.0	59	9-6	4.2	84	11-7	6.3
10	6-11	—	35	8-4	3.1	60	9-7	4.3	85	11-9	6.5
11	7-0	—	36	8-4	3.1	61	9-8	4.4	86	11-11	6.6
12	7-1	—	37	8-5	3.2	62	9-9	4.4	87	12-0	6.8
13	7-2	—	38	8-5	3.2	63	9-9	4.5	88	12-2	6.9
14	7-3	—	39	8-6	3.3	64	9-10	4.6	89	12-4	7.1
15	7-3	—	40	8-6	3.3	65	9-11	4.6	90	12-6	7.2
16	7-4	—	41	8-7	3.3	66	10-0	4.7	91	12-7	7.3
17	7-5	—	42	8-7	3.4	67	10-0	4.8	92	12-9	7.4
18	7-6	—	43	8-8	3.4	68	10-1	4.8	93	12-10	7.5
19	7-7	—	44	8-8	3.5	69	10-2	4.9	94	13-0	7.7
20	7-7	2.2	45	8-9	3.5	70	10-3	5.0	95	13-2	7.9
21	7-8	2.2	46	8-10	3.6	71	10-3	5.1	96	13-4	8.0
22	7-8	2.3	47	8-10	3.6	72	10-4	5.1	97	13-6	8.2
23	7-9	2.4	48	8-11	3.7	73	10-5	5.2	98	13-8	8.3
24	7-9	2.4	49	9-0	3.7	74	10-6	5.3	99	13-11	8.5
25	7-10	2.5	50	9-0	3.8	75	10-7	5.4	100	14-2	8.7

Reprinted by permission of Houghton Mifflin Co.

EXHIBIT 2

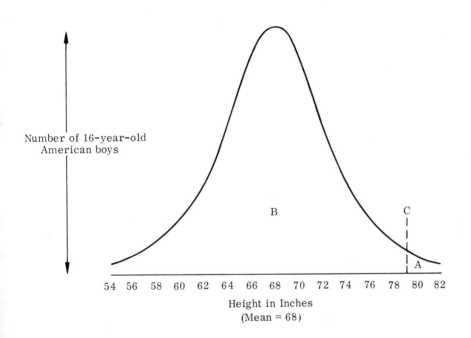

Number of 16-year-old
American boys

B   C

A

54 56 58 60 62 64 66 68 70 72 74 76 78 80 82
Height in Inches
(Mean = 68)

EXHIBIT 3

A.

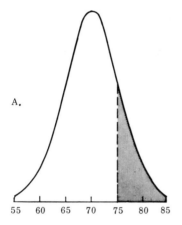

B.

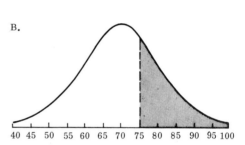

EXHIBIT 4

Percentile Equivalents of Standard Scores

Standard Deviations above the Mean	Percentile Rank	Standard Deviations below the Mean	Percentile Rank
+3.0	99.9	-0.0	50.0
+2.9	99.8	-0.1	46.0
+2.8	99.7	-0.2	42.1
+2.7	99.6	-0.3	38.2
+2.6	99.5	-0.4	34.5
+2.5	99.4	-0.5	30.8
+2.4	99.2	-0.6	27.4
+2.3	98.9	-0.7	24.2
+2.2	98.6	-0.8	21.4
+2.1	98.2	-0.9	18.4
+2.0	97.7	-1.0	15.9
+1.9	97.1	-1.1	13.6
+1.8	96.4	-1.2	11.5
+1.7	95.5	-1.3	9.7
+1.6	94.5	-1.4	8.1
+1.5	93.3	-1.5	6.7
+1.4	91.9	-1.6	5.5
+1.3	90.3	-1.7	4.5
+1.2	88.5	-1.8	3.6
+1.1	86.4	-1.9	2.9
+1.0	84.1	-2.0	2.3
+0.9	81.6	-2.1	1.8
+0.8	78.8	-2.2	1.4
+0.7	75.8	-2.3	1.1
+0.6	72.6	-2.4	0.8
+0.5	69.2	-2.5	0.6
+0.4	65.5	-2.6	0.5
+0.3	61.8	-2.7	0.4
+0.2	57.9	-2.8	0.3
+0.1	54.0	-2.9	0.2
+0.0	50.0	-3.0	0.1

EXHIBIT 5

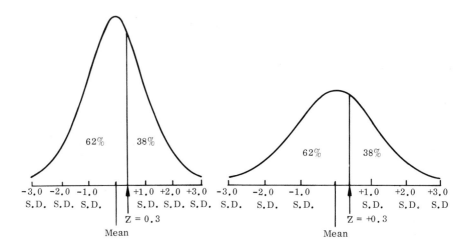

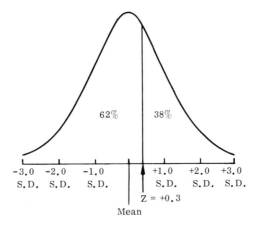

EXHIBIT 6

Distribution of Deviation I.Q.'s

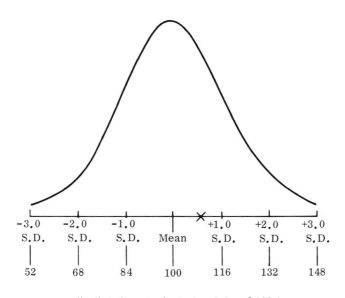

("x " indicates deviation I.Q. of 108)

Exhibit 7

THE LORGE – THORNDIKE INTELLIGENCE TESTS

LIST REPORT OF PUPIL SCORES

EAST HIGH   FORM 1   LEVEL G   GRADE 10

TEACHER GREEN

NAME OF PUPIL	GRADE	DATE OF BIRTH		AGE		VERBAL						NONVERBAL						TOTAL IQ
		MO	YR	YRS	MOS	RAW SCORE	IQ	GRADE %ILE	AGE EQUIV YRS	MOS	GRADE EQUIV	RAW SCORE	IQ	GRADE %ILE	AGE EQUIV YRS	MOS	GRADE EQUIV	
ANDREWS LISA S	10	03	52	15	06	051	109	70	17	06	118	37	103	54	16	02	106	106
BROWN TERRY A	10	12	51	15	09	065	121	91	18	06	121	55	127	96	18	06	124	124
CARLSON ELIN E	10	04	52	15	05	047	105	60	16	06	108	54	127	95	18	06	124	116
DYLHOFF LAPRY D	10	12	51	15	09	045	102	54	16	01	104	42	109	69	17	10	124	106
FOX SANDRA L	10	02	52	15	07	045	103	54	16	01	104	36	102	50	15	10	102	103
GORLA RONALD T	10	12	51	15	09	061	117	87	18	06	121	47	115	82	18	06	124	116
HANSON DAVID A	10	07	52	15	02	057	116	81	18	06	121	45	115	77	18	06	124	116
IVERSON CONNIE S	10	09	52	15	00	044	105	52	15	11	102	28	95	28	14	00	86	100
JENSON LINDA D	10	09	52	15	00	061	121	87	18	06	121	61	141	99	18	06	124	131
KEENA JEANETTE M	10	11	51	15	10	065	121	91	18	06	121	53	124	94	18	06	124	123
MOULTON TIMOTHY R	10	02	52	15	07	061	118	87	18	06	121	47	116	82	18	06	124	117
NORTON PHILIP J	10	12	51	15	09	056	112	79	18	06	121	52	123	92	18	06	124	118
NUTLEY DEBBY S	10	03	52	15	06	065	122	91	18	06	121	54	127	95	18	06	124	125
OLSEN RICKY LEE	10	10	52	14	11	047	108	60	16	06	108	49	122	87	18	06	124	115
PETERSON NORMA C	10	09	52	15	00	050	111	67	17	03	115	45	116	77	18	06	124	114
RALSTON CHRIS R	10	04	52	15	05	043	101	49	15	08	101	49	119	87	18	06	124	110
SWARTZ GARY T	10	12	51	15	09	040	98	41	15	02	96	43	110	72	18	02	124	104

Reproduced by permission of Houghton Mifflin Co.

EXHIBIT 8

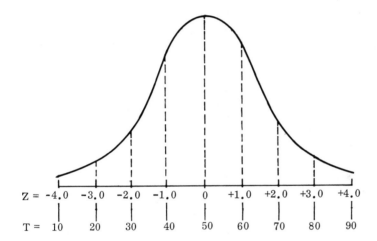

EXHIBIT 9

Scores on "Hypothetical Test of Intellectual Ability" Compared with High-School Grade Averages

Student No.	HTIA Score	Grade Average
1	35	82
2	31	74
3	42	90
4	46	88
5	29	78
6	31	86
7	40	70
8	48	96
9	34	92
10	25	74
11	21	66
12	29	64
13	33	72
14	37	80
15	32	70
16	46	94
17	24	80
18	30	82
19	37	76
20	39	74
21	43	76
22	28	72
23	36	80
24	35	68
25	30	70
26	24	72
27	27	62
28	42	84
29	34	82
30	21	72

EXHIBIT 10

Data from Exhibit 9 Portrayed Graphically

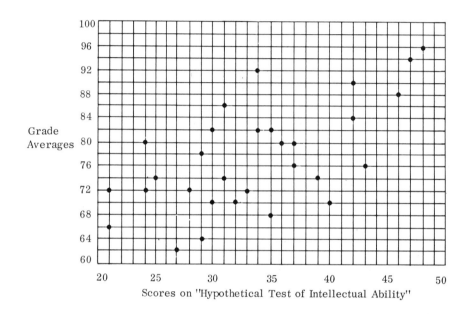

EXHIBIT 11

Data from Three Additional Students Added to Exhibit 10

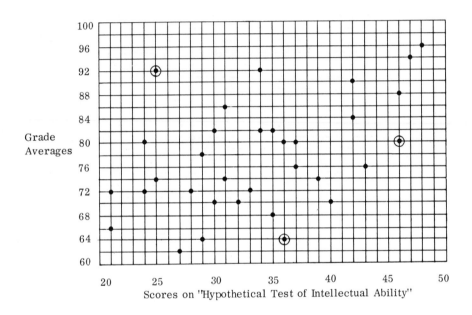

Scores on "Hypothetical Test of Intellectual Ability"

EXHIBIT 12

Correlation Coefficients for Selected Variables

Variables	Correlation Coefficient
Heights of identical twins	.95
Intelligence test scores of identical twins	.88
Reading test scores grade 3 versus grade 6	.80
Rank in high school class versus teachers' rating of work habits	.73
Height versus weight of 10-year-olds	.60
Arithmetic computation test versus nonverbal intelligence test (grade 8)	.54
Height of brothers, adjusted for age	.50
Intelligence test score versus parental occupational level	.30
Strength of grip versus speed of running	.16
Height versus Binet IQ	.06
Ratio of head length to width versus intelligence	.01
Armed Forces Qualification Test scores of recruits versus number of school grades repeated	−.27
Artist interest versus banker interest	−.64

From R. L. Thorndike and E. Hagen, Measurement
and Evaluation in Psychology and Education, 3rd ed.,
© 1969, John Wiley and Sons, Inc., New York, p. 158.

EXHIBIT 13

Validity of Selected Tests as Predictors of Certain Educational and Vocation Criteria

Predictor Test	Criterion Variable	Validity Coefficient
Lorge-Thorndike Intelligence Test (Verbal)	*Iowa Tests of Basic Skills (Total Score —Gr. 4)*	.78
American College Testing Program Test Index	College Grades—English	.54
	College Grades—Math	.44
Seashore Tonal Memory Test	Performance test on stringed instrument	.28
Short Employment Test		
Word Knowledge Score	Production index—80 bookkeeping machine operators	.10
Word Knowledge Score	Job grade—106 stenographers	.53
Arithmetic Skill Score	Production index—80 bookkeeping machine operators	.26
Arithmetic Skill Score	Job grade—106 stenographers	.60
Differential Aptitude Tests (Grade 8)		
Verbal Reasoning	English grades 3½ years later	.57
Space Relations	English grades 3½ years later	.01
Mechanical Reasoning	English grades 3½ years later	.17

From R. L. Thorndike and E. Hagen, Measurement and Evaluation in Psychology and Education, 3rd ed., © 1969, John Wiley and Sons, Inc., New York, p. 170.

EXHIBIT 14

Test–Retest Reliability Study: Hypothetical Test of Intellectual Ability

Student No.	First Score (September)	Second Score (November)
1	35	38
2	31	37
3	42	40
4	46	48
5	29	27
6	31	26
7	40	41
8	47	46
9	34	30
10	25	22
11	21	25
12	29	31
13	33	39
14	37	36
15	32	30
16	46	40
17	24	21
18	30	38
19	37	41
20	39	38
21	43	45
22	28	32
23	36	37
24	35	33
25	30	34
26	24	26
27	27	28
28	42	45
29	34	27
30	21	23

EXHIBIT 15

Test–Retest Data (from Exhibit 14) Portrayed Graphically

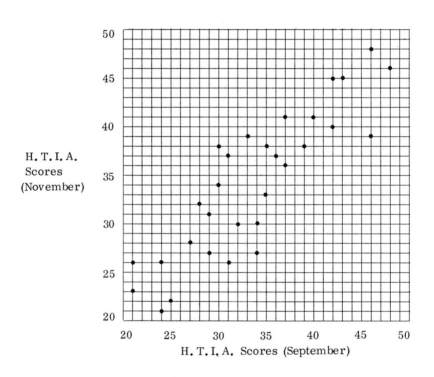

H. T. I. A.
Scores
(November)

H. T. I. A. Scores (September)

EXHIBIT 16

Percentage of Correct Decisions When 50% of a Group Is to Be Selected and 50% Rejected

Validity Coefficient between Test and Criterion	Percentage of Correct Choices*
.00	50
.20	56
.40	63
.50	67
.60	71
.70	75
.80	80
.90	86

*Rounded to nearest whole number

T Scores

1.   A standard score converts any raw score into a score that represents the number of standard deviations (in either direction) away from the mean. A z score is only one kind of standard score that is used. The main advantage in using it is that the score actually states the number of standard deviations from the mean.

    The z scores have the practical disadvantages, however, of using minus numbers, using decimal points, and being confined in a very small numerical range. Thus the difference between, say, +0.2 and +0.6 sounds like very little but actually represents the difference between the 58th and 73rd percentiles.

    A T score has the same meaning as a z score but without these disadvantages. The average T score is 50. This corresponds to the mean, or to a z score of 0. Ten points in a T score correspond to one standard deviation. This is shown in the diagram in Exhibit 8 (page 133). From the above information or from Exhibit 8, a T score of 60 would correspond to a z score of _____.

- -

+1.0 (one standard deviation from the mean)

2.   To convert from a z score into a T score:

(1) Multiply z by 10 (because 10 points in a T score corresponds to one standard deviation.)
(2) Add 50, because 50 in a T score is equivalent to the mean.
(3) As a rough check, visualize where both the z score and the T score would be in the normal curve diagram.

EXAMPLE 1

If the z score is +0.3, what is the T score?

(1) 0.3 times 10 = 3
(2) 3 + 50 = 53
(3) In the diagram in Exhibit 8, note the point that represents a z score of +0.3 and a T score of 53.

EXAMPLE 2

What is the T score that corresponds to a z score of -2.1?

(continued)

Step 1: =2.1 x 10 = -21
Step 2: =21 + 50 = +29
Step 3: (Optional) You can verify for yourself, using Exhibit 8, that a z score of -2.1 is equivalent to a T score of 29.

EXAMPLE 3

What is the T score that corresponds to a z score of -1.4? (Try this one yourself.)

_____

_____

_____

- -

36
10 x -1.4 = -14;   -14 + 50 = 36   (You might want to verify in Exhibit 8 that a z score of -1.4 is equivalent to a T score of 36.)

3.   This is the formula for the computations you have been doing:

$$T = 10z + 50$$

To get from a T score to a z score, the formula is:

$$z = \frac{T - 50}{10}$$

EXAMPLE 4

If the T score is 73, what is the z score?

(1) 73 - 50 = 23
(2) 23 ÷ 10 = +2.3
(3) If you like, verify in the diagram that a T score of 73 is equivalent to a z score of +2.3.

EXAMPLE 5

If the T score is 44, what is the z score?

_____

_____

_____

-0.6
(44 - 50 = -6; -6 ÷ 10 = -.6)

4.   To find the percentile rank indicated by a T score, simply convert it into a z score and look up the percentile in Exhibit 4.   What percentile rank is indicated by a T score of 58? Use the formula in the preceding frame; then use Exhibit 4 (page 129).

_____

_____

_____

- -

79th percentile

$$z = \frac{58 - 50}{10} = \frac{8}{10} = +0.8;$$ from Exhibit 4, this is the 79th percentile

5.   Many textbooks provide tables to convert T scores into percentiles. If you don't have access to such a table, you can't go wrong by converting the T score into a z score and then using the table in this book. Practice in working back and forth between T and z scores is helpful in understanding the standard deviation, the normal distribution, and other statistical concepts discussed in this book.

Glossary

Age equivalent: See equivalent scores.

Alternate-form reliability: The degree to which two equivalent forms of the same test give results that are consistent with each other, as measured by a reliability coefficient. The form and level of difficult of the items are supposed to be the same; only the content of the items changes.

Average: In general, the single number that "typifies" or "best describes" a set of data. See also mean and median.

CEEB score: The type of standard score used in tests administered by the College Entrance Examination Board. The mean is equal to 500 and the standard deviation equal to 100.

Confidence interval: A range of values within which we are confident, at some preestablished level of certainty, that the true value lies. The greater the degree of desired certainty, the larger the confidence interval must be.

Construct validity: The degree to which a test measures some quality or ability that is actually a meaningful entity. In mental-ability testing, this often resolves in practice into a question of whether or not a test is actually testing something other than general intelligence.

Content validity: As used in this book, the degree to which a test is a representative sample of items. More generally, the degree to which the test itself actually measures what it purports to measure.

Correlation: The degree to which two measures are associated with each other, as measured by a correlation coefficient. A positive correlation means that there is some relationship; a negative correlation, an inverse relationship; no correlation, no relationship.

Correlation coefficient: A numerical measure of a correlation, usually given to two decimals. A correlation of $+1.00$ represents a perfect positive correlation; 0.00, no correlation; -1.00, perfect negative correlation. If no plus or minus sign is given, the coefficient is assumed to be plus. See also reliability coefficient and validity coefficient.

Criterion: An indication of real-life performance that a test is supposed to predict or that can serve as a check on a test. Sometimes a criterion can be another test, but in any case it must be something other than the test in question. (Plural: criteria)

Criterion-related validity: The degree to which test results correlate in the predicted direction with external criteria. Sometimes referred to as "predictive validity" or "empirical validity."

Deviation IQ: A standard score used for tests of general intelligence in which the mean is 100 and the standard deviation usually is 16 (15 in the Wechsler scales). These numbers were chosen so that scores would be comparable with <u>ratio I.Q.</u> scores.

<u>Equivalent scores</u>: The age or grade in a standardization sample for which the average score is closest to a raw score in question. It is "equivalent" to nothing and tells us little or nothing about the person that we do not already know from comparing him with his own <u>reference population</u>.

<u>Face validity</u>: The extent to which a test appears to be valid just by looking at it. This bears no necessary relationship to any of the genuine aspects of <u>validity</u>.

<u>Fatigue effects</u>: Deterioration in performance that may result from a test being taken more than once.

<u>Grade equivalent</u>: See <u>equivalent scores</u>.

<u>Intelligence quotient</u>: See <u>ratio I.Q.</u>

<u>IQ</u>: As generally misused, a synonym for general intelligence. Correctly used, IQ has no meaning at all except as a kind of <u>standard score</u> used on intelligence tests. See also <u>deviation IQ</u> and <u>ratio I.Q.</u>

<u>Mean</u>: The average value as computed by adding all numbers and dividing by the number of items.

<u>Median</u>: The "middle" value in a set of data. By definition, 50 percent of all scores fall above the median and 50 percent fall below.

<u>Measurement error</u>: The degree to which a given result differs from the "true" result that would be obtained if the measurement were taken an infinite number of times. See also <u>standard error of measurement</u>.

<u>Norm</u>: A statement of how a given <u>reference population</u> has performed on a test, based on computations made on a <u>standardization sample</u>.

<u>Normal Distribution</u>: A mathematical model that is represented geometrically by the bell-shaped curve in which there are relatively few cases at the extremes and many cases as the values approach the <u>mean</u> value. The distribution is symmetrical around the mean. It is assumed that most human characteristics are distributed "normally," although this assumption is often one of convenience rather than established fact.

<u>Observed score</u>: The score or result that a person attains on one given occasion as distinguished from the <u>true score</u>.

<u>Odd-even reliability</u>: The most frequently used method of ascertaining <u>split-half reliability</u>. The odd-numbered items are considered one subtest and the even-numbered items as another.

<u>Percentile rank</u>: The percentage of persons in a given <u>reference population</u> whose score is below a given score. For example, if a score is in the 65th percentile, 65 percent of all scores in that <u>reference population</u> are below it.

<u>Practice effects</u>: Improvement in performance due to taking a test, or even the same kind of test, more than once.

<u>Ratio I.Q.</u>: An index of intelligence computed by dividing a person's mental age score by his chronological age. To avoid working with decimals, the quotient is multiplied by 100. This method has not been used since 1960. Scores obtained by this method are generally comparable with <u>deviation IQ</u> scores.

<u>Raw score</u>: The number of points scored on a test. Without other information it tells us nothing.

<u>Reference population</u>: Persons sharing one or more specified characteristics such as age, grade in school, geographical location, or sex.

Comparisons are meaningful only when made within a specified reference population.

Reliability: The degree to which a test gives consistent results on different occasions or when different items are used. See also alternate-form reliability, split-half reliability, and test-retest reliability.

Reliability coefficient: A correlation coefficient that expresses the degree of reliability of a test. The higher the coefficient, the more reliable the test. Reliability coefficients should be in the .80's or .90's for tests of well-researched, stable abilities.

Split-half reliability: Any method, of which odd-even is the most common, of dividing a single test into two equivalent subtests. The split-half method is used as a less costly and more convenient substitute for the alternate-form method of estimating reliability. Since each half of the test will be shorter than the total test, the complete-test reliability is underestimated by the correlation coefficient between the two halves, necessitating the use of a correction formula.

Standard deviation: The square root of the sum of the squared deviations from the mean divided by the number of elements less one. This is the best mathematical representation of the variability around the mean.

Standard error of measurement: A quantity equal to the standard deviation of the test multiplied by the square root of $1 - r$, when r is a reliability coefficient. In approximately 95 percent of all cases, a person's true score will differ from his observed score by no more than two times the SEM in either direction.

Standardization sample: The historical group of subjects on whom the test norms were computed and who provided evidence in reliability and validity. All norms that ostensibly are comparing a student with a general reference population are in fact comparing him literally with the persons in this sample, who are assumed to be representative of the population at large.

Standardized test: A published test which has norms data and evidence of validity and reliability, as computed on the basis of a standardization sample.

Standard score: A type of score in which raw scores are expressed in terms of some number of standard deviations away from the mean. Any numerical values can be assigned to correspond to the actual (raw) mean and standard deviation. See also CEEB score, deviation IQ, T score, and z score.

Test-retest reliability: The degree to which a test will give the same results on different occasions.

True score: The hypothetical score that a person would obtain if he were tested an infinite number of times and the results averaged.

T score: A widely used standard score in which the mean is 50 and the standard deviation is 10. Sometimes T score is used synonymously with standard score, although in fact it is only one kind.

Validity: The extent to which a test actually measures something meaningful (construct validity), is constructed so as to represent faithfully the universe of possible tasks that could theoretically be tested (content validity), and is related to performance outside the testing situation (criterion-related validity).

Validity coefficient: The correlation coefficient between a test and a
criterion.

Variability: The degree to which the elements in a distribution are
"spread out" from the mean. Variability is usually measured by computing the standard deviation.

Z score: A standard score in which the numerical units represent the
actual number of standard deviations away from the mean. About
99.9 percent of all z scores in a given distribution are between −3.0
and +3.0.

Suggestions for Additional Reading

Anastasi, Anne. Psychological Testing, 3rd ed. Macmillan, New York, 1968. This is one of three major textbooks in the field of tests and measurements; Cronbach along with Throndike and Hagen (discussed below) are the others. All three are excellent. Anastasi is the broadest in score, and is recommended for undergraduates who have not yet decided on a special field, or for persons whose interest is industrial testing.

Armore, Sidney J. Introduction to Statistical Analysis and Inference ... for Psychology and Education. Wiley, New York, 1966. This book has been very helpful to the author but, because of its mathematical emphasis, is not recommended for self-instruction outside of a regular course.

Cronbach, Lee J. Essentials of Psychological Testing, 3rd ed. Harper and Row, New York, 1970. One of the major textbooks in the field of tests and measurements. Cronbach is suggested for graduate students of psychology. The mathematically based theoretical conceptions presented here are at the forefront of modern personality theory and research and are indispensable for the serious student of psychology. However, much of Cronbach is unnecessarily difficult for the general reader, who would be better off with one of the other textbooks (or even with Cronbach's own second edition, 1960).

Lyman, Howard B. Test Scores and What They Mean, 2nd ed. Prentice-Hall, Englewood Cliffs, N. J., 1971. Here the mathematical treatment is much more detailed and there is much less emphasis on validity than in Interpreting Test Scores. Lyman can be extremely valuable if the reader is willing to dig in and do some rigorous thinking. Otherwise, the reader may be captivated by Lyman's intelligence and wit but miss the main statistical points.

Payne, David A., and Robert F. McMorris (eds.). Educational and Psychological Measurement. Blaisdell, Waltham, Mass., 1967. This book is a rarity: a group of readings selected with an overall purpose and structure in mind. The result is a well-balanced book with many selections which readers of the present volume will find both useful and comprehensible. The excerpts from the National Committee on Test Standards are especially recommended.

Thorndike, Robert L., and Elizabeth Hagen. Measurement and Evaluation in Psychology and Education, 3rd ed. Wiley, New York, 1969. This is one of the major textbooks in the field of tests and measurements. It is very clearly written and is recommended particularly for teachers, school administrators, and other readers whose interest is primarily education.

Tyler, Leona E.   Tests and Measurements. Prentice Hall, Englewood Cliffs, N. J., 1963 (1st ed.); 1971 (2nd ed.). Tyler's cursory treatment of basic statistical concepts is not likely to be of use to many students, but fortunately these chapters in her book are not a prerequisite to the lucid and helpful overview that follows. (There is very little change between the first and second editions).

Vernon, P. E. (ed.).   Creativity. Penguin Books, Middlesex, England, 1970. This book of readings is recommended for students who are interested in the questions raised in Chapter 4 in connection with creativity. Many of the papers in this volume are already classics in psychological research, although not directly addressed to the interests of the practical educator.

Final Examination

NOTE: Some of these questions require use of the z-score formula on page 32, the percentile-equivalent table on page 129, and the formula for the standard error of measurement on page 114. Except for these references, the most value will be obtained from this test by attempting to answer without looking elsewhere in the book.

1. Elaine, a student in the sixth grade, answers 55 questions correctly (out of a possible 100) on a standardized test of arithmetic skills. Ignoring the issues of validity and reliability, what does this tell us about her arithmetical ability? Explain your answer.

2. In the above example, 55 would be Elaine's:

    _____ raw score
    _____ standard score
    _____ percentile score

3. Elaine's score of 55 would be considered "high" if the mean and standard deviation for all sixth graders were:

	Mean	SD
_____	50	10
_____	45	15
_____	45	5
_____	60	5

4. On a certain test the fourth-grade norm is a raw score of 53. What is the meaning of the word "norm" in this context?

5. Describe briefly how the above norm would have been determined.

6. In the previous examples, we have seen that Elaine, a girl in the sixth grade, has a score that is about two points higher than the norm for students in the eighth grade. Can we conclude that Elaine would do about average work in an eighth-grade arithmetic class? Give reasons for your answer.

7. On a College Board examination, what is the percentile equivalent of a score of 700?

8. On the Stanford-Binet intelligence test, 6-year-old Marvin scores 111 (deviation IQ score). What percentile is this equivalent to?

9. Explain the meaning of the above result as you would to a parent.

10.   Words such as "normal," "superior," "genius," "dull," and
        others are sometimes used in reference to scores on intelligence
        tests. What are some of the pitfalls in using such words?

11.   On a standardized intelligence test, with mean 100 and SD 16,
        Tom's verbal IQ score is 116; nonverbal, 104. Jane's verbal IQ
        score is 104; nonverbal, 120. (Assume that on this test the verb-
        al and nonverbal scores have equal weight in determining total IQ
        score.)
        (a) Who has the higher total IQ score?
        (b) Who is more likely to do well in scholastic subjects?
        (c) Who is more likely to appear to be "brighter" to a teacher?
        (d) Which of the two has a significant difference between verbal
             and nonverbal IQ score?

        _____ Tom
        _____ Jane
        _____ both
        _____ neither

12.   The term "predictive validity" is occasionally used, but is actually
        outdated (for reasons not discussed in the text). If you saw that
        phrase in an article or textbook, you could assume that it refers to
        to:

        _____ face validity
        _____ content validity
        _____ construct validity
        _____ criterion-related validity

13.   A "mechanical ability" test is the subject of a symposium among
        experts in the field of ability testing. Expert A is concerned with
        whether or not the items on the test are well chosen to be truly
        representative of everything that has to do with mechanical ability.
        Expert B is concerned with whether or not the results of the test
        enable employers to predict success in a mechanic's job any better
        than would be predicted by chance. Expert C is concerned with
        whether there is any such thing as "mechanical ability" as opposed
        to specific abilities such as numerical skill, motor coordination,
        spatial visualization, and others that should be tested separately.
        Assume that each of the experts has sufficient research data on
        which to base his analysis.
        (a) Indicate which aspect of validity each expert is concerned
             with. (You may refer to the types of validity listed in the
             previous question.)

        Expert A: _____ validity
        Expert B: _____ validity
        Expert C: _____ validity

        (b) If you were an employer deciding whether or not to use the
             test, which of the three experts would you be most interested
             in listening to?

_____ Expert A
_____ Expert B
_____ Expert C
_____ all three have to be given equal weight

14. Applicants for a bookkeeping position take tests of clerical aptitude, arithmetical skills, and general intelligence. The correlation coefficient between the clerical-aptitude test and the arithme-
tical-skills test is .95. The correlation coefficient between each
of those tests and the test of general intelligence is also .95.
On the basis of the evidence presented, which statements could
reasonably be assumed to be correct?

_____ (1) Persons who did well on the clerical-aptitude test did
not do well on the other tests.
_____ (2) The clerical-aptitude test is a good way to predict job
success as a bookkeeper.
_____ (3) "Clerical aptitude" might be nothing more than a combination of arithmetical skills and general intelligence.
_____ (4) None of the correlations is positive.
_____ (5) A person who scores high on one of the tests is likely
to score high on the others.

15. Which of the above statements (1 through 5) has to do with the
question of "construct validity"?

16. What is most needed in order to prove or disprove statement 2 in
question 14?

_____ validity study
_____ reliability study
_____ careful inspection and analysis of all three tests

17. Reliability primarily has to do with:

_____ whether accurate predictions can be made on the basis of
test results
_____ whether a test will give consistent results
_____ the extent to which a test measures what it purports to
measure

18. A new standardized test of grammar is given to all students in the
seventh grade of a certain school. The test consists of sentences
in which the students are to identify the nouns and verbs, determine whether the sentences are complete, and other tasks based
on comprehension of the grammatical structure of the sentences.
The results turn out to be quite different from what would have
been expected on the basis of what the teachers already knew (or
thought they knew) about the grammatical abilities of the students.
So the school principal decides to conduct a reliability study. He
goes through the test and changes each sentence so that the grammatical analysis is identical, but the content of the sentences is
changed. For example, the sentence "The mouse ran away from
the cat" is changed to "The man ran away from the taxicab." Each
sentence in the test is similarly changed, the idea being that perhaps the urban students were thrown off by nonurban examples.

The following year, the grammar test is given to that year's crop of seventh graders. The testing is split into two sessions. The first time, the students take the original version of the test. The second time, a few weeks later, they take the principal's version.

What kind of reliability study is being undertaken?

_____ test-retest
_____ alternate-form
_____ split-half

19.   Continuing the above example, the correlation coefficient between the two sets of test results (original version and principal's version) turns out to be .89. Assuming that this is a good reliability coefficient, which of the following conclusions could reasonably be drawn?

    _____ (1) If there is any major amount of unreliability in the original grammar test, it does not have to do with the content of the examples.

    _____ (2) The reason that the results of the original test did not turn out as the teachers would have expected is that the examples were biased against students who were good at grammatical analysis but who happened to be unfamiliar with the words used in the sentences.

    _____ (3) Students who do relatively well on one of the tests will do relatively well on the other.

    _____ (4) In changing the examples used, the principal actually made a major change in the test itself which would lead to major differences in results and in interpretation of the results.

20.   The principal remains unconvinced that the original test results were reliable. He recalls that there was a fierce thunderstorm at the time the original test was administered. The four seventh-grade teachers who were in the testing room that particular day all recalled the thunderstorm and all agreed that it obviously distracted the students. But their conclusions from this fact differ, as follows:

Teacher A says that the more reliable a test is, the less the results should be affected by unusual circumstances.

Teacher B says that the thunderstorm would tend to detract from the reliability of the test results because the circumstances favored those who had a strong ability to concentrate on the task independent of actual grammatical ability.

Teacher C says that all students were present at the same time during the same storm so that its effects, if any, would cancel out and therefore not affect the reliability of the results.

Teacher D says that if students were in fact distracted by the thunderstorm, this would show that the test was reliable rather than unreliable, since we would expect that a good test would require the students to be responsive to their surrounding environment.

Which of the teachers is (or are) correct? _____

21.   If we are concerned not with the content of the examples but with the ability of the test to give reliable results irrespective of unusual circumstances, what kind of reliability study should be undertaken? Whichever answer you give, briefly describe what it consists of.

     _____   test-retest
     _____   alternate-form
     _____   split-half

22.   The reliability coefficient of a certain reading comprehension test is .84. The standard deviation of the test is 15 points. Compute the standard error of measurement. (The square root you will need is .4.)

23.   On the above test, Alice scores 82. We can be 68 percent confident that her "true" score on this test is between _____ and _____, and 95 percent confident that it is between _____ and _____. (NOTE: If you were unable to answer question 22, then instead of filling in the blanks, state how you would arrive at the answers once you knew the standard error of measurement.)

24.   What is the meaning of the phrase "true score" in the above example?

25.   Suppose that students who score 90 or above on the test in question 22 are eligible to take an advanced reading program. (Assume that this qualifying score is not arbitrary, but is based on research and analysis of the program and the test.) Based on your answers to questions 22 through 24 (which you may look up if you are not certain of them), which of the following statements might be true?

     _____   (1) We cannot be 95 percent certain that Alice does not qualify for the advanced reading program.
     _____   (2) Another student, Eileen, who scored 91 the same day Alice scored 82 is no more likely than Alice to be qualified for the advanced reading program.
     _____   (3) Eileen's "true" score might actually be lower than Alice's "true" score.
     _____   (4) A test should not be used to determine who gets into an advanced reading program.
     _____   (5) In a democratic society there should be no such thing as an advanced reading program for specially selected students.

ANSWERS TO FINAL EXAMINATION

NOTE: The numbers in parentheses indicate chapter references for those readers who wish to review.

1.   Nothing. We have no way of knowing whether this is a poor score or a fine score for a sixth-grade student. (1)

2.   Raw score. (1)

3.   Mean 45; standard deviation 5. Elaine's score of 55 would be two standard deviations above the mean. (2)

4.   53 is the average score obtained by students in the eighth grade on this test. (The answer to avoid is that 53 is what an eighth-grader "should" score.) (1)

5.   The test would be given to large numbers of students in the eighth grade (along with students in other grades) chosen to be representative of the entire country. This group would be known as the "standardization sample." (1)

6.   You should not conclude that Elaine can do eighth-grade work in arithmetic. All we know is that her score in this test on that particular day was about the same as the average score of eighth-graders. But she may have been able to score many points without having to know some of the concepts taught in the seventh and eighth grades. She could therefore be much better than eighth-graders at elementary arithmetical operations, but nowhere near their ability in problem-solving. (1)

7.   98th percentile

$$z = \frac{X - \overline{X}}{s} = \frac{700 - 500}{100} = +2.0$$

From Exhibit 4, this equals a percentile rank of 97.7, or 98. (2)

8.   76th percentile.

$$z = \frac{X - X}{s} = \frac{111 - 100}{16} = \frac{11}{16} = +0.7$$

Percentile rank equals 75.8, or 76. (2)

9.   Marvin's score on this test was higher than 76 percent of all scores achieved by persons of his age. If he were tested on another occasion he might be several points lower or several points higher. We are interested less in the number itself than in the range it may seem to indicate, and it is certainly reasonable to say that the result is at least average or above average. The important point to remember is that we are talking about the results, not the child himself. (See below for continuation of this answer.) (3)

10.   We can make statistical statements about a score on the basis of theoretical and actual knowledge, but there is no justification for applying labels to the child himself on the basis of the score. However, words such as "normal," "superior," "genius," "dull," etc. often sound as if they were meant to describe the child himself. Moreover, the cut-off point between one range of scores and another range is completely arbitrary. The child might score below the cut-off on one occasion and above on another. (3)

11.   (a) Jane. (Her average of verbal and nonverbal was 112; Tom's was 110. The question assumes that each of the components had equal weight.)

        (b) Tom. Verbal IQ is more related to school work than nonverbal IQ.

(c) Tom, for the same reason. Teachers see the result of verbal intelligence and they also get some first-hand observation of the processes of linguistic and arithmetical reasoning. But they rarely get a chance to observe nonverbal intelligence at work.

(d) Jane. When the two scores (verbal and nonverbal) of a single individual are one standard deviation apart or more, it can be considered statistically significant. The standard deviation was given as 16, and the difference between Tom's verbal and nonverbal scores was only 12. (3)

12. Criterion-related validity. (4)

13. (a) Expert A: content validity
Expert B: criterion-related validity
Expert C: construct validity
(None of the experts had anything to say about face validity, since they were arguing on the basis of research data rather than just by an impression of what the test looked like.) (4)

(b) Expert B. If there are solid data to prove that the results actually predict success in a mechanic's job, an industrial employer doesn't really care too much about the theoretical issues raised by Experts A and C. Similarly, if the test results do not predict who will do well on the job, it makes no difference how valid the test may be from various theoretical points of view. (4)

14. Statements 3 and 5 are correct.

The first point to recognize is that .95, even though the plus sign is omitted, is a very high positive correlation. This means that statement 4 is incorrect, and that by definition statement 5 is correct. Statement 1 is therefore incorrect.

Statement 2 is incorrect in that no evidence was presented for job success (see question 16). Moreover, it may well turn out that even if clerical aptitude is highly correlated with success as a bookkeeper, one of the other tests might prove to be a better predictor than the clerical aptitude test.

Statement 3 might be correct, especially when we bear in mind the fact that the test is called something does not necessarily mean that such a thing exists. If clerical aptitude had a much lower correlation with these other two abilities, we might have more reason to believe that it actually exists as something separate from arithmetic skills and general intelligence. (4)

15. Statement 3. (4)

16. Validity study. (A careful inspection and analysis will tell us nothing about the ability of the test to make accurate predictions.) (4)

17. Whether a test will give consistent results. (5)

18. Alternate-form. (In a test-retest study, the identical test would be given again to the same students. In a split-half study, the test would be administered only once without any alternate form being constructed.) (5)

19.   Statements 1 and 3 are correct. The latter follows directly from
        the very high correlation coefficient. Since students who did well
        on one form of the test tended to do well on the other, and the only
        major difference was in the content of the examples, we can as-
        sume that this really did not make a major difference. The sec-
        ond statement is what the principal originally thought, but that
        simply didn't turn out to be the case. The fourth statement is in-
        correct, since the alternate form clearly did not lead to major
        differences in results. (5)

20.   Teacher A is correct. This is one of the definitions of reliability.
            Teacher B is also correct. When we test a certain ability we
        want the results to reflect that ability only and no others.
            Teacher C is incorrect. The effects of unusual circumstances
        do not "cancel out"; on the contrary they affect some students
        more than others. Extraneous factors detract from the actual
        ability that the test is designed to measure.
            Teacher D is indulging in a bit of whimsy--or nonsense, if you
        prefer. (5)

21.   Test-retest. The identical test is given to the same students at
        a later time. The students are the same, the test questions are
        the same, so the only thing that may change is the motivational
        factors and even physical factors having to do with success on a
        particular day. (The ability itself is presumed not to change over
        a short period of time.) (5)

22.   SEM equals 6 points.

$$\text{SEM} = s\sqrt{1 - r}$$
$$= 15\sqrt{1 - .84}$$
$$= 15 \times .4 = 6.0 \quad (6)$$

23.   68 percent confident: between 76 and 88; 95 percent confident:
        between 70 and 94. (The observed score was given as 82 and the
        SEM was computed to be 6 points.)
            Verbal answer: for 68 percent confidence, add and subtract one
        SEM from the observed score in both directions. For 95 percent
        confidence, add and subtract two SEM's from the observed score.
        (6)

24.   The "true" score is the score that a person would obtain if tested
        an infinite number of times and the results averaged (with no prac-
        tice or fatigue effects intervening). (6)

25.   Statement 1 is correct, because in question 23 we computed that
        at the 95 percent confidence level there is some possibility that
        Alice's "true" score is as high as 94.
            Statement 2 is incorrect. Eileen's "true" score might be below
        90 and Alice's "true" score might be above 90. But it is more
        likely that Eileen's score is higher than Alice's, since the results
        on one occasion provide the best estimate we have.
            Statement 3 is correct. It was not necessary actually to calcul-
        ate the 95 percent confidence interval around Eileen's score, since
        it was shown in question 23 that Alice's "true" score might be as
        high as 94.

Statements 4 and 5 may be correct, but there is no way to answer them from the evidence presented in the questions themselves. One of the purposes of this book is to enable the reader to distinguish between conclusions that are based on evidence and conclusions that are based on personal opinion and guesswork. The latter kind of conclusion may well be just as good or even better than the former, but it is important to separate the two types. In this question, then, only statements 1 and 3 should be considered correct. (6)

Index